Cases of Identity

Cases of Identity

Being the Real People in the Sherlock Holmes Canon

By
David L. Hammer

Illustrated by Paul Churchill

Gasogene Books
INDIANAPOLIS

GASOGENE BOOKS
An imprint of Wessex Press, LLC
P.O. Box 68308
Indianapolis, IN 46268

Copyright © 2006 by David L Hammer.
All rights reserved.

No part of this publication may be reproduced, stored in a retrieval system, or transmitted in any form or by any means, electronic, mechanical, photocopying, recording, or otherwise, without prior written permission of the author and publisher.

ISBN 0-938501-45-3

Printed in the United States of America.

1 3 5 7 6 4 2

First Edition

This book is dedicated to
AGNES REECE HAMMER

A REMARKABLE MOTHER,
WHO ALWAYS ENCOURAGED HER YOUNG SON
TO JOURNEY TO CARCHEMISH AND SAMARKAND

"My dear fellow," said Sherlock Holmes as we sat on either side of the of the fire in his lodgings at Baker Street, "life is infinitely stranger than anything which the mind of man could invent."
— "A Case of Identity"

"The world is full of obvious things which nobody by any chance ever observes."
— *The Hound of the Baskervilles*

"For strange effects and extraordinary combinations we must go to life itself, which is always far more daring than any effort of the imagination."
— "The Red Headed League"

Contents

Foreword ix

1 The Sorcerer 1
2 The Sorcerer's Apprentice 7
3 The Hero 10
4 The Heroine I 23
5 The Heroine II 32
6 The King 38
7 The Queen 48
8 The Judge 56
9 The Villain 68
10 The Maiden 80
11 The Premier 90
12 The Prince 100
13 The Duke 107
14 The Devil's Apprentice I 114
15 The Devil's Apprentice II 120
16 The Valley of Vermissa 127
17 The Exodus 156

19 The Great-Hearted Soldier 162
20 The Connecticut Connection 169
21 The Literate Portrayer 180
22 The Moonlight Portrayer 185
23 The Myth.................................. 190

Afterword 193
Bibliography................................... 196

Foreword

IF, as Sir Francis Bacon opined, every lawyer was a debtor to his profession, so also is every hobbyist to his hobby. In that spirit I have researched and written this little book, and I can only hope that it will return something to the Sherlockian community from which I have, through the years, received so much.

Contrary to my wife's claim that I am by nature a recluse, which I deny; I do however admit to being a closet solitarian, although I do enjoy some companionable moments. A discussion and a drink with an old friend can be a delight, and indeed, under the august authority of everyone's late and wise friend, John Bennett Shaw, so also may a drink alone. Still, my interest is not in Holmesian badges or attending seemingly endless meetings, but in Sherlockian search and research and recording the results. The other Holmes, O.W. Jr., wrote about the secret isolated joy of the solitary thinker, but that isn't my bag either; I prefer the pleasure of the literary chase, the capturing of an insight, the cornering of a clue, the attainment of a different view of something, and to find a relation perhaps unrecognized by others. These activities continue to remain my particular delights, and if creation is godly, as one can plausibly maintain from the essential attribute of God, then to the extent we mortals create, whether a song or a symphony, a cabbage or a child, a prize poem or a prize pig, we are partaking in something holy.

Just as I believe that Doctor Doyle, who was an indefatigable traveler, whether on foot or bicycle or on those horrible huge Victorian tricycles, was always looking for places to match the stories which he carefully crafted in advance, so am I also abidingly convinced that he saw in real places the sites which he selected for his yarns. The proof of this theory as to places I've tried to establish in my *Game* books. It is therefore a corollary truth that he must have done the same with real people. That theory I have sought to present here.

I must acknowledge certain debts to prior writings of mine. Where I have already written something which is relevant, I would prefer to use it, rather than paraphrase what has been previously crafted. Thus I have used certain chapters from *To Play the Game* regarding James McParland and one chapter from *The Before Breakfast Pipe* about the King of Bohemia, which was first published in the *Sherlock Holmes Journal*, all of which sources I herewith credit.

So *Fanget an!* Let us begin. Together we will explore the matching of real people with canonical characters, and perhaps find a parallel or two or even a counterpart. Can't you already hear that distant *view halloo?*

DAVID L. HAMMER
March 1st, 2005
St. David's Day
Laurel Cottage
Dubuque

Cases of Identity

The Sorcerer

THE SORCERER can only be one man — Mr. Sherlock Holmes himself; he who made magic. And he was one of the magi, for what fictional character has more books written about him? I am advised that the number totals even more than Christ, and Christ is a tough act to follow.

Holmes, like that slightly earlier fictive character, Frankenstein, is a construct. Most of Holmes' living tissue, like that of his colleague, Dr. John H. Watson, came from the living soul of Arthur Conan Doyle, failed doctor, veritable polymath, avid discoverer, thoroughgoing gentleman, and always an outsider looking inside as befits a writer. He was a man with many causes, and to each he offered his integrity, his fidelity and an untrammeled honesty. There was no treachery, no dissemblance, no disharmony, in the man Doyle. He possessed an abundance of convictions, and he acted upon every one of them, usually to his serious disadvantage. Few mysteries passed him by — except the Whitechapel Murders, for some unknown and arcane reason, which must remain inexplicable until his family ceases to fight over the treasure in his papers. He was a seeker, and a successful one, intent with Holmes—intensity upon unravelling even the slightest nuance and subtlety of mystery, as well as the greatest one of all.

This last observation suggests a man possessed of logic bounded by reason yet with the uncanny ability to not only obtain the measure and bounds of others, but to place himself within their psyche. Remember Holmes' compliment to Watson that he never got his measure?

Surely any explanation of Doyle's life is redundant: those who read him already know it, and those who don't won't be reading this book. Many who write cannot effectively function outside their fiction. They accomplish by their characters what their character cannot do. It is successful sublimation, and the more successful, the more profitable, in money and recognition. Doyle was able to function quite successfully beyond his books, and it was the man rather than the author which was the more remarkable work. The phrase which continues to appear unbidden to my fingers is that of a gentleman unafraid, for he made himself a gentleman, in the purely English sense of the term, and if he was fearful, his triumph over it was all the greater for its apparent nonappearance. He took on tough projects, from the Boer War to insisting upon suitable military preparations in advance for what was later called The Great War. And he was inventive, from the concepts of body armor for soldiers to the creation of territorial armies to observations about the prospective but fearful powers of submarines over a sea-girt kingdom.

Not content with taking on the powers of the military and government as to preparedness, he fought to a victory the cases of Edalji and Slater, both of whom were as unpopular and un-English as were the protagonists. Probably the most unpopular cause of all was that of Sir Roger Casement, an Irish hero who made common cause in wartime with the King's enemies, the Imperial German Empire. Doyle, who opposed Home Rule for Ireland, fought hard but without avail against the prosecution and ultimate execution of Casement, which was complicated by Casement's homosexuality. Doyle had known of his reportorial work on the abuses in the Belgian Congo, which was a cause both of them supported.

Doyle was not tolerant of homosexuality, which he regarded as a sickness, but he did not drop his friends for that reason; in fact, he supported them in the face of much invective. Oscar Wilde was a friend and Michael Harrison once told me that one of Wilde's sons advised him that during Wilde's incarceration in Reading Gaol Doyle helped support the Wilde family. There was nothing showy about Doyle, nothing done which was not the result of bedrock integrity, and he had no truck with bad means for good ends than good means for bad ends.

Twice he stood for Parliament, and twice he lost. It must have been doubly disappointing for he stood for principle, but I suspect he lacked the ability to kowtow to the electorate. He was direct rather than deceitful. Certainly England was the loser.

Holmes' capacity for reasoning was abstracted from Doyle's own exceptional rationality, but the essential trick of the thing was owed to Doyle's preceptor, Dr. Joseph Bell, who had the uncanny knack of drawing startling conclusions from immediate observations. Medicine teaches careful and precise observation, and even as late as Doyle's day, the clinician was obliged to rely upon his observations as opposed to the diagnostic machine marvels of today. Doyle was taught, as had generations of doctors before him, that different diseases offered different smells, and these were part of the then classical clinical armamentarium.

DR. JOSEPH BELL

Doyle had many occasions, as Dr. Bell's clerk, to watch him in clinical contexts, to file away Bell's obervations, and thereafter withdraw them when it came time to write the Holmes stories, adapting the process from a medical to a detective context. Indeed, they added an essential verisimilitude to the Holmes persona.

It should be noted that the egalitarian drab of our democracies has destroyed most of the outward Victorian clothing differences, with the dress of most people today being substantially indistinguishable. Doyle, Bell and Holmes would have a much more difficult time today.

If we believe Doyle, then we must accept that Dr. Joseph Bell was indeed, a substantial portion of the persona of Sherlock Holmes, for in 1892 Doyle acknowledged that, writing from his new home in South Norwood to Dr. Joseph Bell, in material part, as follows:

> My dear Bell,
>
> It is most certainly to you that I owe Sherlock Holmes Round the centre of deduction and inference observation which I heard you inculcate, have tried to build up a man who pushed the thing as far as it would go — further occasionally — and I am so glad that the result satisfied you, who are the critic with the most right to be severe.[1]

Yet that was a recognition compounded of appreciation and veneration, and was a bit to simplistic, for while the role of Bell in the creation of Mr. Holmes was mightily significant, it was measurable. Bell was the offeror of the method which became known as the Sherlockian method, and which was a consequence of a clinician's extremely perceptive observation and a capacity for shrewd inductive reasoning. The method was the very essence of the Holmes mystique, and without it, he would have been a very pale character.

Who was Joseph Bell? He was a medical doctor, the scion of a long line of medical doctors, born in 1838 into a cultured and privileged Edinburgh family. He obtained his medical degree from the University of Edinburgh in 1859 and continued to be associated with that institution in one way or another for the rest of his professional life. He was a sportsman, an avid long distance walker — ten miles being a routine tramp — and was an active member of the Free Church of Scotland, which meant in essence that he was a committed Presbyterian who attended two services each Sunday. His religion played a large role in his life and he did far more than sit in the Amen corner.

In one of those Koestlerian coincidences which abound

in matters Sherlockian, Bell married into the famous Murray family, who furnished to Doyle young Murray, the Hero of the Canon. Her name was Edith Murray, and was a daughter of the eighth Baron of Elibank. She was an exemplary wife and mother, giving her husband much happiness in their married life, which unfortunately ended before their middle years. The shock of her death caused his jet black hair to turn white virtually overnight. He never remarried and was a fine father to his several children, all of which testified to his deep feeling for his dead wife.

He wrote on medical matters, with both his *Surgical Manual* and *Nurse's Manual* going through many editions. He was one of those who worked for the entrance of female nursing students into the Medical School, which was accomplished, but in separate classes. He was also interested in graphology, which he believed evidenced personality and character traits. He received most of the medical honors which his profession could offer, but for us the most significant aspect of his professional life was the offer to the young Doyle to be his dresser, that is, medical assistant, an honor which surprised Doyle, but which became an incalculable opportunity to closely observe Bell.

The Bell stories are legion but have been written about so often that further exemplification is tedious. Let it be sufficient to relate the medicine episode, which was his much repeated teaching tool to emphasize the importance of observation. He would take a bottled liquid with an offensive taste, place a finger inside the bottle and thereafter put a different finger to his lips. The students, nonobservant all, would accept his offer to taste the liquid, and each grimace from that taste. Then Bell would observe that the finger which he put in the liquid was different from that which he placed in his mouth.

Bell had always regarded Doyle as one of his best students; in later years sent Doyle a picture of himself which Doyle kept on his mantel,[2] and he wrote the introduction to the 1892 edition of *A Study in Scarlet*, which was a fulsome tribute to both Holmes and Doyle.

Unlike Conan Doyle, in 1888 Bell interested himself in the Whitechapel murders, and perhaps effected a solution. According to Bell, he and a friend each considered the known facts, the suspects, and where their researches intersected found the murderer. Each man wrote the name of the murderer on a sheet of paper, then exchanged them, and the same name was apparently on each. Bell notified Scotland Yard of the name and it is reported that a week later the murders ceased. This is interesting speculation but even Holmes would discount it, rendering the Scottish peculiar third verdict of not proved.

Robert Louis Stevenson, another native Edinburgher, was also admired by Doyle, who sent him a book of Holmes stories. Stevenson wrote back "Only one thing troubles me: can this be my old friend, Joe Bell?"[3] We already know that in a significant part, it was.

NOTES

1. Liebow, Ely M., *Dr. Joe Bell, Model for Sherlock Holmes* (Bowling Green University Popular Press: Bowling Green, OH, 1982), p. 172.
2. Page 175, *Ibid.*
3. Page 174, *Ibid.*

The Sorcerer's Apprentice

IF THE SORCERER was Mr. Sherlock Holmes, and it was, then the sorcerer's apprentice can only be Dr. John H. Watson. The inquiry must be as to whether there was an original from which Watson was drawn. There have been several candidates, some not unexpectedly known by the patronymic of Watson. There is Patrick Heron Watson, a contemporary of Joseph Bell, and both professors at the University of Edinburgh. Watson was the leading surgeon of the day, known for his lightning swift ability to amputate a limb, a technique much admired by doctors and much appreciated by patients in the days before anesthetics. He was a veteran of the Crimean War, for wars breed surgeons, and when young Doyle was a student he could choose between Drs. Bell and Watson for the courses in clinical surgery. We know that his choice rested on Bell, but that does not militate against Patrick Watson as the original in being or in name of Dr. Watson.

There was also Dr. James Watson of Southsea, where Doyle practiced, but Jay Finley Christ, that superb Sherlockian scholar, established that Doyle did not know Dr. James Watson until subsequent to the time he wrote *Study in Scarlet*.

I have been guilty of offering another Dr. John H. Watson, the real name of the clergyman who wrote under the *nom de plume* of Ian Maclaren.

Unhappily, we know that none of the above constituted the original John H. Watson, for the original was in truth and in fact, Ormond Sacker. But you will protest that even if Watson was the second name selected, there still had to be an original. That may well be correct, but theoretically we should be looking for the original of Ormond Sacker, and thusfar no one has followed that rather obvious lead.

But we must not confuse the name with the persona. Doyle could well have drawn the name from one source and the character from quite another. For example, at Stonyhurst, which young Doyle attended, there still remains a desk with "A. Watson" carved on it, with the miscreant's full name being Alfred Aloysius Watson. Additionally, there are many Watsons abounding still around Stonyhurst. As for the name, we cannot go further than Doyle's statement in his *Memories and Adventures*, that he required "a drab, quiet name for this unostentatious man. Watson would do."

What about the persona of Watson? Cuthbert B. Smith, a resident of Des Moines in the period from 1938 until 1943, was the son of an English doctor who had been a fellow student of Doyle at Edinburgh University Medical School, wrote an article for the *Des Moines Sunday Register* issue of January 16, 1938, in which he asserted, without any attendant proofs, that his father, William Smith, was the paradigm for Doctor Watson. It is an interesting proposal, but it lacks any probative evidence, so it may be summarily dismissed.

The short and accurate answer is that Doyle was Watson, just as another part of him was Holmes. Doyle did not think like Watson but he looked like him and he understood him, sufficiently so that he could create a believable character; so believable in fact that he entered literary immortality.

Watson posessed Doyle's rock-ribbed integrity, and each could be counted upon to do the ethical and honorable thing, even at the risk of failure or misperception.

There was one person who recognized Watson in Doyle, and he had some knowledge of Watson. Remember when Doyle met William Gillette for the first time? The celebrated meeting occurred at the Hindhead Railway Station, near Doyle's home. When they saw each other, each in open-mouthed astonishment exclaimed only two words: Doyle said "Sherlock Holmes" and Gillette said "Dr. Watson." We could do much less than accept William Gillette's identification.

The Hero

The hero in the Holmes Saga is, of course, young Murray.

> There stood the gallant Murray,
> The pride of Tullibardine,
> Who saved the wounded Watson
> For the honor of their Queen.

There is no personage in the entire Canon more wholly creditable than he who deserves the accolade of the gallant Murray.

Watson not only recognized that he owed his life to the gallant orderly, but even after the fact was willing to publicly acknowledge it.

Watson carefully noted his debt early on in the first page of *Study in Scarlet*: "...I served at the fatal battle of Maiwand. There I was struck on the shoulder by a Jezail bullet, which shattered the bone and grazed the subclavian artery. I should have fallen into the hands of the murderous Ghazis had it not been for the devotion and courage shown by Murray, my orderly, who threw me across a pack horse, and succeeded in bringing me safely to the British lines."

It reads like an Old Testament litany, and is probably the most famous story line in the entire Canon.

The borrowing of the name of Murray is not accidental, for there is no name more famous in the annals of Scotland than that of Murray or Moray. It is a name which still fires Scottish spirits, for Murray courage was legend, and when the Murrays were cut down their bodies were found by the side of their king, whether it be of Scotland or England. Whether fighting for or against the English crown, and they did both, but at ethically divisible points in time and family, they were acknowledged to be superb warriors.

One of the major clans, whether subdivided into the green tartan of Atholl or the red of Tullibardine, the Murrays left their mark on Scotland.

Some years ago, visiting Holyrood Palace in Edinburgh[1] with my Murray partner,[2] we chanced upon an old portrait in the place of honor above the fireplace in the Queen's dining room. It was a fierce old warrior with the legend beneath the portrait simply stating, Sir Mungo the Murray[3] which meant that he was once head of the clan. I do not know to this day how he came to be so valued by the German rulers of England, but he had the look of a fighter, and one who would most cheerfully rend asunder an adversary with one stout blow from his claymore.

The Murrays were acquirers of power, not deliberately, but in consequence of appreciation by the sovereign for their war-prowess, and with power came titles, and more titles. Through the years they became the dukes, earls and marquesses of Atholl, earls and marquesses of Tullibardine, lords of Elibank, baronets of Clermont, viscounts of Stormont, lairds of Falahill, earls of Streathern, earls of Dunmore, and the holders of some eleven baronetcies. In addition, they were the sovereigns of the Isle of Man and the holders of the Barony of Strange, surely a most sinister holding. They were also clerics, one of whom, the bishop of Caithness, became Saint Gilbert, and judges, one of whom was Lord Mansfield, who became the founder of English commercial law.

The Murrays, one of the most feared of Scottish clans, were fabled warriors in a country which produced fabled warriors. No one, and particularly their enemies, ever accused them of being less than wholehearted; in one battle alone, four generations of Murrays gallantly perished.

So gallant Murray, although an orderly and not a lowland chief, could be expected to be at Maiwand, fighting for his queen.

Doyle, who was himself a Scotsman, born and bred in Edinburgh, did not select the name of Murray for Watson's orderly randomly. As a student of history from his childhood he could hardly have avoided the testy and brave Clan Murray.

* * *

The Murrays were founded by one Freskin, a Pictish nobleman, who was granted feudal rights by Scottish King David I in the Moray province in the tenth century, deriving his new patronymic from the name of his new province. The feudal rights included the castle known as Duffus.

The grandson of Freskin, Sir William Murray, obtained the estate of Tullibardine by marriage in 1286, and in 1443, Sir David Murray, the seventh laird, was granted the barony of Tullibardine. Sir John Murray, the twelfth laird, obtained an earldom from James VI of Scotland, who subsequently became James I of England. William Murray, the second earl, married the daughter of the Earl of Atholl, who were members of the royal Stuart family, and their son John became the first Murray Earl of Atholl.

John, a royalist, was captured by the Roundheads in 1640, and was taken to Edinburgh as a prisoner, being released on the payment of a large fine and an undertaking to furnish and lead a regiment in the Roundhead army. His son, John, was also a royalist, and was so in a time during Cromwell's Protectorate when only the brave and foolish adhered to the crown. He unsuccessfully sought to rescue Charles II in 1650, thereafter rendering his submission to London; however three years later he led an uprising of Highlanders, bringing two thousand men to the Stuart colors. This revolt also failed, but after the Restoration he held many important posts, becoming Marquess of Atholl in 1676.

John's brother, and the second remarkable son of the Earl, was Lord Charles Murray (1661-1710), a soldier who fought in the Flanders campaign in 1684. James II created him the first Earl of Dunmore. Three of Dunmore's sons became generals and fought for England. The second Earl of Dunmore, John Murray, fought as a young ensign at Blenheim in 1704 and as an old general at Dettingen forty years later. The third earl fought for the rebels in the Rebellion of 1745, but was later pardoned.

Another John, the fourth Earl of Dunmore, (1732-1809), was the royal governor of New York and Virginia during the beginning of the American Revolution. He unsuccessfully fought the Virginians, firing the city of Norfolk. Disappointed, he returned to England in 1776, taking with him his unpopularity with the Colonists.

As for the Atholl connection, John, the marquess, (1666-1724), was created the Duke of Atholl 1703, and it became a family custom for the first son of the duke to bear the title of Marquess of Tullibardine, which has continued to this day. John, his eldest son, was killed in the battle of Malplaquet in 1709.

The first duke supported the government in the Jacobite uprising in 1715, but Murrays fought on both sides of that rebellion, which the Scots still term "the rising." William,(1689-1746) The Tullibardine successor to his elder brother, John, ultimately died as a political prisoner in the Tower. He fought for the Jacobites in 1715 at the battle of Sheriffmuir, which resulted in his attainder, so that his younger brother became the next in line for the dukedom. William fled to France, still loyal to the Stuart cause, returning to Scotland in 1719 in command of a Stuart expeditionary force, but after the defeat at Glenshiel he fled again to France.

It was the final Jacobite uprising in July of 1745 which caused the severest split in the Clan Murray. William returned from France with Bonnie Prince Charlie, being honored by reading the royal proclamation and unfurling the Stuart standard. Lord William's father, the duke, fled from his seat at Blair Castle, whereupon Lord William entertained the prince there. In the subsequent invasion of England, William commanded many of the Jacobite forces, but the insurgency ended disastrously at the battle of Culloden in April, 1746. William was captured and died in the Tower.

One of Lord William's brothers, Lord George (1694-1760), had also served the same Stuart cause in the Rebellion of 1715, fleeing to France after its failure, and living in poverty. He returned to Scotland in 1719 for that uprising and was wounded in the battle of Glenshiels. Escaping again to France, he returned when his father, the duke, obtained a pardon for him; unfortunately, his brother, William, prevailed upon him to join in the rebellion of 1745. Lord George was appointed a lieutenant general and it was generally agreed that he became "the soul of the undertaking."

Lord George carried the day at the battle of Prestonpans, and in the subsequent invasion of England, captured Carlisle. There were few English recruits to his forces, requiring the army to retreat to Scotland, and Lord George commanded the rear so successfully that the entire army escaped back there.

At the battle of Falkirk, Lord George commanded the right wing of the Jacobite forces, which battle was conducted in a January storm, full of fierce winds and pelting rain. He fought in the front of the battle, leading his troops on foot, brandishing his sword. His orders to his troops were not to fire until the enemy was within twelve paces. This tactic broke the English charge and caused a pandemonic retreat by the enemy.

Later, in seeking to gain Blair Castle, the Murray family seat, his small force of twenty-four men was attacked by greatly superior numbers of English troops. Placing his men behind a turf wall, at widely spaced intervals, he ordered his banners to be waved and the pipers to play with vigor. He confounded the English, who swiftly retreated to the castle, believing they were faced with vastly superior numbers. The castle was then invested by him, but just before the surrender he was called to Culloden. Despite the Murray courage there, the Scots were decimated and the Stuart hopes were forever ended.

Although the cause was lost, it was said by Chevalier Johnstone in his *Memoirs*, that "had Prince Charles slept during the whole of the expedition, and allowed Lord George Murray to act for him according to his own judgment, he would have found the crown of Great Britain on his head when he awoke."

Lord George escaped to the Continent, dying in 1760 in Holland. Of his three sons, John became the third Duke of Atholl, George a vice admiral, and James a major-general, who was injured in such a manner as to be ever after unable to lie down.

James, the first Duke of Atholl's third son (and brother of Lords William and George), became the second Duke of Atholl. He pursued the Jacobites as the captain-lieutenant of the King's footguards, and by inheritance obtained the sovereignty of the Island of Man and the barony, among others, of Strange.

The fifth son of the first duke was Lord Charles (1691-1720), who served as a cornet in Flanders in 1712 and 1713, and joined his brothers, William and George, in the 1715 uprising, commanding a regiment in the battle of Prestonpans; captured, he was ulltimately pardoned at the instance of his father.

Lord John Murray (1711-1787) a son of the first Duke's second marriage, was a professional soldier for the English king, ultimately becoming a general, but he was proudest of his forty-two years as the colonel of the 42nd Highlanders, famed as the Black Watch. He was intensely loyal to his men, and the "papers of the day speak of him as marching down in full regimentals at the head of the many highlanders disabled at Ticonderoga in 1758, to plead their claims before the Chelsea board, with the result that every man received a pension."[4] Additionally, he offered a cottage rent free at his estate, Banner Cross in Yorkshire, to any man disabled from his service in the 42nd Highlanders.

We have discussed two branches of the Murray clan, but there are others in addition to the Dunmores and the

Atholls. There are the Murrays of Falahill, the Clermonts, the Elibanks, the Stormonts, the Philiphaughs and the Ochtertynes, all equally distinguished in the arts of war.

John Murray (died 1510), the seventh laird of Falahill, claimed descent from Archibald of Moravia, who swore allegiance to Edward I in 1296, and whose son, Roger obtained the Falahill estate in 1321. The seventh laird of Falahill was a fearsome subject of the ancient and well-known border ballad about his taking possession of the Ettrick Forest in Selkirkshire, claiming to hold it "contrair all kings of Christentie."[5]

King James IV confronted him with a large force and a deal was struck that in exchange for the sheriffship of the forest Murray would submit fealty to the king. Sir Walter Scott wrote that the tradition "bears that the outlaw was a man of prodigious strength, possessing a baton or club, with which he laid lee the country for miles around, and that he was at length slain by Buccleugh, or some of his clan, at a little mount covered with fir trees, adjoining Newark Castle..."[6]

Sir James Murray (1751-1811), was the seventh baronet of Clermont, with a seat at Fifeshire. His mother was the daughter of the fourth Lord Elibank, so he was a Murray on both sides of his parentage. A professional soldier, he was first gazetted to the North American colonies under Lord Cornwallis in 1775, and was involved in expeditions to South Carolina and New York. In 1778 he commanded a battalion at the capture of St. Lucia in the West Indies, and thereafter returned to England in 1780. In 1793-4 he was, as a major general, in Flanders with the then Duke of York.

Shot in the North Holland campaign, he was reputed to have chuckled at now "having been shot through both arms and both legs."[7] His last campaign was in Spain during the Peninsular War. Later he was Secretary of State for War and died in 1811 from the consequences of an explosion of a powder flask.

He married wealthily in 1794 to Henrietta Pulteney, Baroness Bath. Her father was regarded as the richest commoner in the kingdom, and by agreement Sir James assumed the name of Pulteney. It was noted that he possessed an "absurd manner and a grotesque and rather repulsive exterior,,,(but) in point of natural abilities he took first rank. He had seen a great deal of the world and of military service, he had read much and variously, and possessed a great fund of knowledge and considerable science. Remarkably good-tempered and unpretending, he was utterly indifferent to danger and to hardship."[8]

Sir John Murray (1768?-1827), the eighth baronet of Clermont, began as an ensign in the Scots Guards and saw action in Flanders in the wars against France. He was involved in the capture of the Cape of Good Hope in 1796, then he took his regiment to India, seeing action there until 1805. In 1809 he fought under the Duke of Wellington in the Portuguese campaign, being mentioned in dispatches for the Battle of the Douro. Wellington reported Murray to be "a very able officer, but…disposed not to avoid questions of precedence."[9] In 1813, as a lieutenant general he was fighting in Sicily, but disobeying orders, was court-martialed on Wellington's instructions, who remarked that Murray lacked "what is better than abilities, that is, sound common sense."[10] He was acquitted of almost all of the charges, and as the remaining ones amounted to a mistake of judgment, he was admonished. The Prince Regent dismissed the admonishment.

The Murrays were also Lords of Elibank, and easily the most distinguished of that group was James Murray (1719?-1794), the fifth son of Alexander, the fourth Lord Elibank. He served with the 15th Foot as a commissioned officer in the West Indies, Flanders and Breton. It was reported that "these services included the Cartagena expedition and subsequent operations in the east of Cuba, the defense of Ostend in 1745 by a mixed force or British and Austrians…and the L'Orient expedition of 1748. At L'Orient Murray was captain of the grenadier company of the 15th, which attacked the French with great gallantry when many of the other troops shamefully misbehaved."[11] In 1751 he purchased a lieutenant colonelcy and took the 15th Foot to Canada. At the investment of Louisburg, the commander, General Wolfe, wrote of him: "Murray, my old antagonist, has acted with infinite spirit. The public is much indebted to him for great services in...advancing this siege."[12]

He commanded one wing in the silent and hazardous climb up the Quebec bluffs and in the ensuing and decisive battle on the Plains of Abraham, Wolfe used him for "the most hazardous exploits of the campaign."[13]

After the surrender of Quebec City, Murray was appointed commander, and with reduced forces he withstood the winter siege until it was lifted the following spring. With the French cession of Canada in 1763 he was appointed governor of Canada, which office he held until 1766. In 1772 he was made a lieutenant-general and two years later was designated as governor of Minorca, which was besieged in 1781 by a combined force of 16,000 French and Spanish troops. Murray's forces were only 2,216, many invalided and infirm. The siege continued until the next year when Murray's troops were reduced to 600 men, most of them being grievously afflicted with scurvy, and Murray surrendered.

Court-martialled, but acquitted of all serious charges, his reprimand was ordered expunged by the King who "was pleased to approve the zeal, courage and firmness with which General Murray had conducted himself in the defense of Fort St. Philip, as well as of his former long and approved services."[14] Murray was described inconsistently during his court-martial as "looking very broken...and quite the old soldier."[15]

His son, Major General James Patrick Murray, received a substantial wound at the Battle of Douro in 1809, which disabled him, dying a few days before his father. One of the ancient Greeks lamented that in war, fathers buried sons. This circumstance occurred again and again in the Murray Clan.

Sir George Murray (1759-1819), a member of the

younger offshoot of the Elibank branch of the Murray family, was one of the few who opted to fight on the seas rather than on the land. As a junior officer, he participated in 1776 in some North American naval engagements, and later against the French fleet. He was captured on the Breton coast after his ship was lost, remaining a French prisoner of war for two years, but productively utilizing his imprisonment to learn French. Repatriated, he served on warships in the East Indies, where he was wounded in action. By 1797 he was captain of a line vessel of seventy-four guns, and participated in the Battle of Cape St. Vincent. Subsequently he was involved in the attack on Copenhagen, having "a brilliant share in the battle."[16] A captain of the Mediterranean fleet, he was later promoted to vice admiral.

Adam Murray (d. 1700) was descended from the Murrays of Philiphaugh in Selkirkshire, but was born in Northern Ireland, the emigration point of many Scots. He grew up in Ling, some nine miles from Londonderry, and at the time the Ulster Protestants rose in 1688 he led his neighbors as a mounted group. When Londonderry was invested by the Jacobite forces under King James II, the town offered to make him governor, but he declined. During a truce the next day the king's representative entered the town and offered Murray one thousand pounds sterling and a colonelcy, which he also declined.

There were periodic sallies from the besieged town and on the first of these, Murray killed the French general with his sword. In the course of the siege Murray played an active role, sustaining serious injuries to his head, and later he was shot through both thighs.

As the city continued to hold, the reputation of Murray increased, so much so that it was then written:

> "The name of Murray grew so terrible
> That he alone was thought invincible:
> Where'er he came, the Irish fled away."[17]

After four months the siege was raised by the arrival of

Prince William's troops, and in appreciation for his brave efforts, Murray was given a pocket watch by the Prince, but declining a pension, he returned home to Ling. He was the modern equivalent of Cincinnatus.

Another branch of the Murrays were those whose seat was at Ochtertyne in Perthshire, at Crieff They produced another George Murray — Sir George, (1772-1846) — who epitomized the warlike qualities of the Clan. Receiving an ensign's commission, he served in the Flanders campaign in 1793, participating in the battles of Famars, Lincelles, and Lammoy, and the sieges of Dunkirk and Valenciennes. In 1799 he was wounded in action in the Netherlands, and later in Egypt he was in several battles as well as the investment of Cairo and Alexandria. Thereafter he was a member of the expeditions to Hannover, the Baltic, Denmark, and Portugal. In the latter expedition he was involved in four battles and was commended in dispatches. He was also in the engagements of the Pyrenees, Niville, Nive, Orches and Toulouse.

Murray went on to become a general, then the governor of Canada, head of the Royal Military College at Sandhurst, a privy councillor, and a member of Parliament.

While the memory of the Murrays is largely military, the spirit of their family manifested itself in other significant ways. Three examples should suffice.

James Murray (1732-1782), a clergyman, was the author of *Sermons to Asses*, published in London in 1768, and dedicated to "the very excellent and reverend Messrs. GW, JW, WR, and MM," noting that "there are no persons in Britain so worthy of a dedication of a work of this kind as yourselves." The GW was George Whitfield, the Quaker, and the JW was John Wesley, the Methodist.

Sir James Murray (1788-1871), a medical doctor, discovered fluid magnesia and first recommended electricity as a curative agent.

William Murray (1705-1793), the son of David Murray, the 5th Viscount of Stormont, became a King's

Scholar at Westminster School and subsequently studied at Oxford's Christ Church. He later was a Bencher at Lincoln's Inn, and a lawyer. Alexander Pope was his close friend, and as a member of Parliament he become a leader of the House. His strongest enemy, Horace Walpole, in referring to one of Murray's speeches, concluded that he "never heard so much argument, so much sense, so much oratory united." Ultimately he became the Earl of Mansfield, who sat from 1756 until 1788 as Chief Justice of the Kings Bench. Singlehandedly, he developed English commercial law. In the Gordon Riots of 1780 his home was burned, along with his significant library. He and his wife escaped out a rear door in the very nick of time. Yet when he presided over the treason trial of Lord George Gordon, who instigated the riots, he was so scrupulously fair that the defendant was acquitted.

It is now time to leave the Murrays and their determined ways. A strong race abundantly possessing both the integrity of honesty and the grace of vitality, their causes were always for issues apart from themselves and they served their kings well and truly. Scotland the Brave, yes, and Murray the brave, also yes.

* * *

But as with most things which begin with Mr. Sherlock Holmes, they also end with him. In this instance, John Murray (1778-1843), a descendant of the Murrays of Atholl, became a London bookseller at 32 Fleet Street, and ultimately the founder of what became a famous publishing company, still existent today. It was the John Murray firm which became the publishers of the two volumes of Holmes stories, known in England simply as the Long Stories and the Short Stories.

So it is that there was significance in Doyle's selection of young Murray as the hero who saved Watson at the Battle of Maiwand.

NOTES

1. Incidently, it was the father of Sir Arthur Conan Doyle who designed the ornate well in the first courtyard of the palace.
2. Angela Murray Simon, the finder of Pondicherry Lodge and the country cottage of the wife of the Missing Three Quarter.
3. Mungo was a Scottish saint, whose first name became a common Scottish given name.
4. p. 1204
5. *Dictionary of National Biography*, p. 1275.
6. *DNB*, p. 1276
7. Bunbury's *Narrative of Passages in the Late War With France*, London, 1854.
8. Bunbury, *Ibid*
9. *Ibid*, p.1286.
10. *Ibid*, p. 1287.
11. *Dictionary of National Biography*, p.1270.
12. *Ibid*, p1270.
13. *Ibid*, p. 1271
14. *Ibid*, p. 1272.
15. *Ibid*, p. 1272.
16. *Ibid*, page 1259.
17. *Ibid*, p. 1241

The Heroine I

THE HEROINE in the tales of Mr. Sherlock Holmes is she whom the sorcerer always referred to as The Woman. That woman he identified as Irene Adler, but we know that, like others in the Canon's populace, this was pseudonymous.

She was woman in all her manifold ways; the woman which all men choose; one who was essentially mysterious, supportive and supplicating yet still strong, but not too strong so as to cease to be comradely; the intriguing giver of all good gifts, and the receiver of all that man can give. She was an experienced and attainable woman, certainly no maidenly shrinking Violet. She was, after all, sensual, for she was The Woman.

JERSEY LILY

If Doyle did not identify her, tradition has identified her. It has not been by common consent — nothing is subject to such agreement in matters Holmesian — but the most popular candidate is Lillie Langtry, the Jersey Lily, who delighted many men and charmed an English king. Her biggest supporter as Irene Adler has been Michael Harrison, who had a particular interest in the *demi-mondaine*. One of his books, provocatively entitled *Fanfare of Strumpets*,[1] discussed these ladies of the evening, who were always sensual, always interesting, usually elegant, and mistresses of their craft, which was more than being sexually attainable, however important that must have been, and may still be.

There is less information vouchsafed about Mme. Adler than most every woman in the Canon, and many of far less consequence; after all, she was Holmes' *the* woman. Now that omission is deliberate and surely significant; however its significance remains shrouded in mystery. We are not even told what she looked like. As to her background we know only that she was born in 1858 in New Jersey, sang as a contralto in Milan's *La Scala* and Warsaw's Imperial Opera House as the prima donna, retiring in an undisclosed year to London. The implication of Count von Kramm's remarks suggested that she was a courtesan, although in Doyle's carefully constructed world there was never anything with even the slightest suggestion of sexual improprieties, much less the existence of such categories of people as "fallen women." His was the world of a gentleman, in every sense and nuance of the word.

Emilie Charlotte le Breton was born on the Isle of Jersey[2] in 1853, the tomboy daughter of the Anglican Dean of the island. Her nickname was Lillie and she became known internationally as the Jersey Lily. Generally regarded as the world's most beautiful woman, she spent her early life living on Jersey and yearning for the abundance of the great world beyond. She later described her deliverance. "One day there came into the harbor a most beautiful yacht. I met the owner and fell in love with the yacht. To become the mistress of the yacht I married the owner, Edward Langtry."

At her insistence they later moved to London, where she learned that her husband's only income came from an allowance from his father. Moreover, he was not interested in social activities (for which she yearned) but preferred hunting and fishing. They obtained quarters at Eaton Place — not to be confused with wealthy Eaton Square — where ultimately they received an invitation to a posh party, and Lillie wore her sole party dress, a simple black affair. Her beauty was primarily a beautiful skin and bone structure with blue eyes and Titian hair. She was almost immediately surrounded by several well-known artists, John Everett Millais, Lord Frederick Leighton, and James Abbott McNeill Whistler. Frank Miles, a young artist and not regarded as being of the same artistic stature, was also there, and on the spot he sketched her on a tailor's bill, which was reproduced and almost overnight copies were hawked all over London. She was instantly famous and while the other artists each did distinguished portraits of her they did not establish her fame as a beauty but only confirmed it. Edward Burne-Jones, George Frederic Watts, Dante Gabriel Rossetti and Edward John Poynter also painted her Pre-Raphaelite beauty.

Millais referred to her as "the most beautiful woman on earth," and in *Iolanthe* Gilbert wrote of her:

> Oh, never, never, never, since we joined the human race
> Saw we so exquisitely fair a face.

It was inevitable that the Prince of Wales would be drawn to her — which I trust is a delicate way of expressing the matter — and in 1877 he had a house built for her in fashionable Bourne-mouth. Carved inside on the panelling was the notation: "They say - What they say - Let them say." On an outside wall was carved *Stet Fortuna Demesis* — which translates as "May fortune attend those who dwell herein."

The Prince treated her quite differently from his other mistresses; he was willing to be seen with her, and she even appeared in the royal box at Ascot and elsewhere with him. In 1880 they spent a holiday together in Paris, dancing at Maxim's, kissing on the dance floor, enjoying the sidewalk cafes and shopping together, or rather, she shopped and he paid. They dined at Victor Hugo's home, who was then 78 years of age, and who optimistically toasted her with the sentiment "Madame, I can celebrate your beauty in only one way, by wishing that I was three years younger."

It quickly became known that if a hostess wished him at a weekend houseparty, Lillie must also be invited. As the

Prince's interest in her increased, her other admirers faded from the scene as did her unhappy husband, who found his only comfort in drinking too much for too long.

What was she like? Michael Harrison didn't like her, referring to one portrait which "makes her almost look like a human being."[3] She has been described by one biographer as ambitious, cold, businesslike and unsentimental.[4]

Harrison is a bit hard on her. I always have admired her, for she made her way successfully, accomplishing what she set out to do; had she been a man, the description just quoted would be regarded as completely complimentary. She triumphed over adversity many times, each time due to her courage and abilities, and she always remained a beautiful and intelligent woman. Indeed, both Oscar Wilde and George Bernard Shaw spoke of her intelligence rather than her beauty. Now the Prince of Wales was not an interesting conversationalist nor even a very bright man, so one cannot regard their relationship as evidencing a recognition of her intelligence, but her life after the breach with the Prince does clearly establish her intelligence and her abilities. William Ewart Gladstone enjoyed her conversation and was sufficiently impressed to become and remain her friend. Perhaps the most significant observation came from Mark Twain: "She doesn't rely on feminine charm. She's what she is, and she is good company with her friends, but it would be hell to be married to her. She's too damn bright."[5] She was also very shrewd, a quality not naturally allied with intelligence. A scurrilous newspaper story claimed, not truthfully, that she had lost both her face and her figure. Those advising her, urged suit, but she refused, observing that "no one sues or contradicts someone who always has the last word."

She and her prince were practical jokers, and at a costume party at the Randolph Churchill's home she slipped some ice down his neck, a *gaucherie* if not *lese-majeste*. He turned, stared long at her, swung around and left the party. Her social invitations immediately ceased, and as she had no other source of income, other than the

Prince's largesse, she determined to go on the stage as an actress. We still have the vestigial phrase, "the legitimate stage," for most actresses were more famous for their activities when not behind the footlights. Her entry on the stage took care of any remaining social standing which she possessed, and her acting was initially amateurish. People did come in droves however to see her and she did show increasing promise, ultimately becoming a classic comedienne and versatile serious actress. Both the Prince and Princess of Wales attended all of her openings, and were both supportive of her, he in assisting her in the theater and she in calling upon her when London society scorned her after the ice episode.

She took *She Stoops to Conquer* to the hustings, and didn't disdain the provincial theater as did most actresses. In Manchester she received twenty-three curtain calls and her carriage was pulled by too enthusiastic fans, resulting in an accident which, fortuitously, damaged neither her person nor her composure. When the play reached London's prestigious Haymarket Theater it was a complete sell-out. From this point forward her income increased and she was never without funds. A good business person, she shrewdly appraised her commercial ventures, and was so successful that writers like Michael Harrison regarded her as greedy. She was the first woman to endorse a product — Pears Soap — which she claimed gave her that famous skin tone, in a written testimonial which was much criticized as being unladylike. Lillie charged one hundred and thirty two pounds sterling for the commercial, which was her weight, since she did not know what to charge.

In the fall of 1882 she and her company came to America. They toured throughout the United States, playing to packed houses everywhere.It was in New York where she met of the significant men in her life, but there were many who were not significant, with whom she became involved. He was Frederick Gebhard, Jr., seven years her junior, and a wealthy Baltimorean. He purchased for her Clement Moore's[6] old home on fashionable 23rd Street as a New

York *pied a terre*, but when she travelled it was on a seventy foot long railroad car made especially to her order.

Despite her developing acting abilities, which had spelled such success for her, she determined in 1883 to study acting in Paris under a famous acting teacher to deepen her now-recognized thespian abilities. There she worked with both Bernhardt and Coquelin, shrewdly writing of the latter, "Coquelin is extraordinary. He says more in a pause than most actors can say in hundreds of words. He drops a hand, he raises an eyebrow, and one feels the controlled powers of his gestures."[7]

Returning to London, she played Lady McBeth, receiving rave reviews, as her craft had deepened. She later took *McBeth* to the United States on tour, in the process becoming an American citizen so that she might more conveniently divorce her husband. She accomplished that without the dreaded but anticipated counterclaims involving her earlier relationship with the Prince of Wales. Her husband, who continued to harbor a certain not unreasonable bitterness, despite the deference to be expected by a subject to his sovereign. Lillie continued his allowance, which remained expressly conditioned on his not contacting her. He was drinking even more heavily now, and was found wandering, dirty, drunk and incoherent in the North of England. He died shortly afterward, on the day that Lillie's horse won the Caesarwitch race at Newmarket.

Her acting career continued apace, with the female leads in both *As You Like It* and *Antony and Cleopatra*, the latter production constituting her biggest hit, earning her a reputed million dollars.

Her friend, Oscar Wilde, paid her a high compliment by writing a play for her in which to star, *Lady Windermere's Fan*, but Lillie refused it because the heroine had an adult illegitimate daughter. It was a closely guarded secret, but in 1881 she had given birth to a daughter, Jeanne, spending what was then termed her period of confinement at Ruthin Castle in Denbighshire. The secret was well-kept, with the daughter being treated as her niece and living during her younger years in Jersey. The natural father was Prince Louis of Battenberg. The daughter married Sir Ian Malcolm in 1902 — her mother giving her away at the fashionable St. Margaret's Church in Westminster. The Malcolm family did not approve of Lillie, and there was a consequent rupture between mother and daughter which persisted for many years.

A catalogue of her sexual affairs would not be as extensive as that of her Continental rival, La Belle Otero (although some clients would be the same) not because she was less active or less publicly promiscuous. Perhaps the difference simply was that she was English.

It is established, or at least as established as one can be in these essentially private matters, that Lillie's royal lovers included Albert Edward, the Prince of Wales, his august cousin, Prince Louis of Battenburg, King Leopold of Belgium, and perhaps Crown Prince Rudolf of Austria-Hungary. Certainly the latter pursued her but she had a not unreasonable aversion to him.

Her real lovers, while rich, were certainly not royal, which speaks to a certain sense of democracy. Freddie Gebhard had passed from her life and thereafter she entered a surprising but torrid relationship with George Alexander Baird, Baron Auchmeddon, a drunken Scottish squire who was a rich roustabout and a boor to boot. None of her friends could understand her interest in him. He gave her blows and bruises, along with a Cartier diamond bracelet, three famous race horses, a 220 foot yacht, all in that order; then, fortuitously, he died. Like all her other possessions, she made the yacht pay, for when she soon tired of the expense she leased it out for the yachting season on a net-net basis.

In 1899, at age 46, she married Hugo de Bathe, who, if he had fewer years, he also had fewer brains, and when his father, the general, died ten years later, she became Lady de Bathe. Like her lovers Gebhard and Baird, he was substantially younger than she, some nineteen years; thus anticipating that ultimate desideratum of the modern woman.

A millionairess many times over, she retired to Monte Carlo in her new home, appropriately named the Villa le Lys, with her husband residing in a house she acquired for him in Nice, and thus did they live happily ever after, apart. She died in Monaco in 1929.

Lillie Langtry was not without vanity, but it had the merit of being an honest vanity. Once she complained to an artist who was giving her a percentage of the sales on prints of a picture of her, that "You have made me pretty, but I am beautiful."[8] During a 1916 transatlantic crossing she and Somerset Maugham conversed, and in the course of that conversation she mentioned the name of Frederick Gebhard. Maugham responded that he had never heard of him. Surprised, she observed that he was the most celebrated man in two hemispheres. Maugham inquired why he was so celebrated, and she responded: "Because I loved him."[9]

* * *

Was Lillie Langtry Doyle's celebrated Irene Adler?

Certainly her credentials are considerable and admittedly they both had a certain correspondence, beyond the birth of Lillie in the Isle of Jersey and Irene in the state of New Jersey. They were both very intelligent and highly spirited courtesans, high-steppers in the nomenclature of the time, and each had appeared professionally on the stage, Lillie as an actress and Irene as an opera singer. Both were vital women, living their lives as they wished, and both were loved by kings. By any test, it is a good match.

NOTES

1. W.H. Allen, London, 1971
2. Undoubtedly the reference to New Jersey as the birthplace of Irene Adler is significant evidence that Mrs. Langtry was the original, as the latter was born on the isle of Jersey.

3. Page 145, Harrison, Michael, *Fanfare of Strumpets*, W.H.Allen, London, 1971
4. Brough, James, *The Prince & The Lily*, Coward, McCann & Geoghegan, New York, 1975
5. Page 165, Gerson, Noel B., *Because I Loved Him, The Life and Loves of Lillie Langtry*, William Morrow and Co., New York, 1971
6. The celebrated author of *The Night Before Christmas*.
7. Page 118, Gerson, Noel B., *Because I Loved Him, the Life and Loves of Lillie Langtry*, William Morrow & Company, New York, 1971
8. Page 166, Brough, James, *The Prince & the Lily*, Coward, McCann & Geoghegan, New York, 1975
9. Page 23, Gerson, Noel B., cited *supra*

The Heroine II

THE HEROINE in literature and art is always a much stronger person than the maiden, and usually neither as naive nor as credulous. For Holmes she was The Woman, and as so characterized, she, by the very use of the term, was no maiden, but a full-blooded, experienced woman, and certainly no timorous, shrinking Violet.

CAROLINE OTERO

While Lillie Langtry remains the favorite filly in the race for Irene Adler, nothing is certain in either harlotry or Sherlockery, and La Belle Otero is gaining good ground. No clergyman's daughter, Caroline Otero was an illegitimate Galician, whose mother, dirt poor, had several other children, all born of different fathers. She was born in 1868 in the town of Valga, in the province of Galicia, in the country of Spain, and beyond this there is very little in her personal history which can be confirmed, largely because of the many varied life stories which she produced on demand. She may have had Gypsy blood, as on occasion she claimed it, and she did perform Gypsy dances, but most assuredly because they were hot-blooded rather than in homage to any putative ancestor. She loved jewelry and gambling, both traits associated with Gypsies, but she did not possess those commonly claimed as Gypsy traits — theft and dishonesty. Except for furnishing inconsistent stories about her childhood, which is easily accountable as wishing to appear interesting, she did not lie and, indeed, her frankness about most things was certainly refreshing, although not refined. She never lost her peasant candor and there were no pretensions to being a lady, as the other successful strumpets of her time were quick to claim. Two of this group of *grande Horizontals* were daughters of the middle class; Lillie Langtry, whom you have already met, and Liane de Pougy, who was the daughter of an officer and who departed school teaching for her new profession with alacrity.

La Belle Otero, for so she was always called, was a dancer in her alternate profession and did some singing, but her voice was not the organ of her success and her dancing evidenced more enthusiasm than grace. She appeared regularly at the Bal Tabarin, where Toulouse-Lautrec sketched, and the Folies Bergere, as well as the Alhambra in London. She danced her way around the world once and appeared in New York several times. In fact, her maiden effort — if that be not an inappropriate characterization — was dancing on the New York stage.

Harrison calls her "one of the most *complete* whores that the world has ever known,"[1] but oddly enough doesn't significantly nor satisfactorily amplify his reasons. Harrison was what was characterized in his day as a man of the world, and it could well be that his pronouncement was intended to be complimentary rather than critical.

Perhaps it will be of some interest to you that two Holmesian authors were entranced with the world of the *demi-mondaine*; Harrison, of course, and also Arthur H. Lewis, who wrote the definitive biography about Otero, entitled *La Belle Otero*.[2] One may speculate endlessly and fruitlessly about whether the interests are cognate or merely compatible, but I suspect that the truth that it is the interest in the time, for the *La Belle Epoch* comprehended the same time frame as did Mr. Sherlock Holmes.[3]

Langtry had grace, and Otero did not. In fact, grace was

never Otero's bag; she peddled unbridled enthusiasm. Her friend, the writer Colette, characterized her breasts as her most distinctive feature, being "of (a) curious shape, reminding one of elongated lemons, firm and upturned at the tips."[4] But it was her eyes which entranced an interviewer from the Philadelphia *Evening Telegram*:

> "Otero's eyes are a deep, lively brown which grow lustrous and brilliant as fiery opals. Her luxurious hair is silky and jet black and falls far below her waist. Her teeth are of perfect shape and look like pearls in her rose bud mouth. Her complexion is as soft and tinted as a peach...her face is of the purely oval Spanish type, and her pretty head is set upon a neck that resembles a column of the whitest ivory."[5]

She was tall for her age and ours; being five feet ten or eleven. Her weight was 138, and the rest of her measurements were 38-23-36.

Her fee was $10,000 per night or jewels in a like amount; we do not know if, like our friend Sherlock, she ever varied them except to omit them. I suspect not, for she had a passion for gambling, and it was conservatively estimated that she lost over $20 million at the Monte Carlo Casino alone. She probably would have lost more there if the wife of the Prince of Monaco, one of her stalwarts, had not banned her from the principality. Otero, as usual, had the last word, declaring that "I didn't want to get Albert into trouble with his wife. She was an ugly bitch and a mean one, too..."

Her customers were the most famous and wealthy in Europe and elsewhere. They included Edward VII, Kaiser Wilhelm II, Tsar Nicholas II of Russia, Prince Nicholas of Montenegro, King Leopold II of Belgium, Prince Albert of Monaco, the Khedive of Egypt, Aristide Briand, the Premier of France, one of the Vanderbilts, and a great many more. She talked about her clientele, observing that "I never thought of them of as kings, only as men." As for King Edward she rather carefully observed "For a man of his age, he was surprisingly virile and generous too."

There were a succession of suicides associated with her,

as it was a popular but serious means of attention. One Christmas morning a Russian count blew his brains out in front of her Paris hotel. Asked by reporters about the matter, Otero replied: "I hardly knew the Count. One night perhaps, certainly no more."

She determined that she wanted to do grand opera, and was careful enough to select *Carmen*, which was Spanish and lively.

Always good copy, her comments concerning whether she was frightened were predictable: "Not a godamned bit! All those smug women witting out there, waiting for me to make a fool of myself; I'd laid half their husbands and the other half would have enjoyed the experience if they could have afforded me. No, I wasn't scared at all." If she lacked culture, and she obviously did, she didn't lack courage.

Michael Harrison noted two examples of her wit and honesty, a deadly combination. "Like all the really great harlots, Otero had a quick and not always charitable wit. To an English banker who was negotiating for her favors she said 'Your money cannot buy my love, but I must admit that it will put you in an excellent bargaining position.'" And when a frustrated man once said to her" 'How can women be so beautiful and yet so stupid?' Otero replied: 'God made us beautiful that they might love us — he made us stupid so that we could love them.'"[6]

I cannot vouch for the accuracy of the following story, but it has been associated with her, as well as one or two other such professional women. Near the end of the last century a number of young French officers, realizing that they were quite unable to afford her charms, even for a few minutes, conceived the idea of a lottery, with the winner receiving the prize money sufficient for an evening with La Belle Otero. It was a stiff price to enter the lottery but it was oversubscribed, and the winner had his evening with her. In the freedom of the bedroom he told her how he had acquired the funds for the evening, and she was quite touched. She asked him how much he had contributed to the lottery, and when he told her, she refunded the money for his ticket.

There was another quality about her which was more engaging than honesty. She was able to avoid jealousy among her gentlemen. In 1898, when she was thirty, five gentlemen met at a posh Paris restaurant to celebrate her birthday. The celebrants virtually represented the *creme de la creme* of the *Almanach de Gotha*; the Prince of Wales, King Leopold II of Belgium, Prince Nicholas I of Montenegro, Prince Albert of Monaco. and Grand Duke Nicholas of Russia. She and they had a delightful time, full of good cheer, if not fun and frolic, although it was doubtful that it was a feast of reason and a flow of soul.

She retired with her beauty and her jewels, but the latter disappeared regularly in exchange for cash on which to live. She spent her last years alone in Nice, in a shabby little housekeeping room in a poor area behind the great hotels in which she formerly stayed. Her gambling beggared her, but she never complained, and she died quietly in 1965, aged ninety-seven, in the process of cooking a rabbit stew.

Irene Adler certainly possessed the spirit of La Belle Otero, but Mme. Adler was far more of a lady, and while both were essentially free spirits, Adler was a far smoother article and more traditional, but then she lacked hot Spanish blood.

Who it was that Doyle had in mind for the original of Mme. Adler, we will never know as a matter of verity, so like most Sherlockian conclusions, it is a matter of individual choice. What could be more democratic?

NOTES

1. Page 151, *Fanfare of Strumpets*, cited *supra*
2. Trident Press, New York, 1967
3. Lewis, by the way, was born and grew up within the confines of the Vermissa Valley, yet he wrote the fairest book about the Mollies which I have ever read — *Lament for the Mollie Maguires*. One of the most pleasant afternoons I ever spent was with him in the small

garden behind his row house in the city of his dreams — Philadelphia. He died within the last few years.
4. Lewis also wrote a great Sherlockian mystery about his fellows in the Sons of the Copper Beeches, not surprisingly known as the Sons of Beeches, and further abbreviated as the sobs.
5. page 4, *La Belle Otero*, cited *supra*
6. Page 4, *La Belle Otero*, cited *supra*

The King

THE KING was the self-styled King of Bohemia. Every fable requires a king and he is ours. Such a king may be good or bad, or both; it is simply sufficient that he is a king.

But king of what? That inquiry is supremely important. As he must be a king in a kingly line, both the appropriate regnal table and the *Almanach de Gotha* must be consulted.

Now we know it to be true that there was a King of Bohemia, many in fact, but the reigning king in the time of our fable was not the individual presenting himself in the sorcerer's chambers that Friday in March in the year 1889. There have been many applicants for the original of that king, and my proposal is that he was the historic Tsar of Bulgaria.[1]

Bulgaria has never received a good press in the United Kingdom, and if one is obliged to defend this thesis, perhaps the ultimate proof is that the verb "to bugger" is a derivative of Bulgar. The term undeniably carries a certain invidious connotation, and if the suggestion be inaccurate, the relationship is etymologically sound. Is it any wonder, then, that Watson, who never chose to produce a *chronique scandaleuse*, substituted a Bohemian scandal for a Bulgarian one? Perhaps no Canonical sub-specialty has been more popular than that of attempting to peel the persona from Wilhelm Gottsreich Sigismond von Ormstein, self-confessed grand duke and hereditary king and his former inamorata, the enigmatic and elegant Irene Adler.

There has been no dearth of royal or even imperial candidates, including the venerable Franz Josef,[2] his ill-starred son the Crown Prince Rudolf[3] and even his intractable nephew Franz Ferdinand.[4] Hapsburgs aside, candidates as disparate as Kaiser Wilhelm II,[5] Edward VII as Prince of Wales,[6] King Milan Obrenovitch IV of Serbia[7] and Prince Alexander of Battenberg, deposed first prince of Bulgaria,[8] have all been proposed.

Unfortunately, close scrutiny reveals improbabilities in each of these attributions.

1. **Franz Josef.** He loved his errant empress despite her disdain for what she characterized as his "sergeant-major soul," and his only known mistress, Frau Kathi Kiss-Schratt, cosseted him with *kaiserschmarren* and domesticity. He may have been the hereditary King of Bohemia, but he was not von Ormstein.

2. **Crown Prince Rudolf.** While women were familiar mysteries to him, and he was involved with a number of the grandest of the Horizontals, he was of slight statute and matched neither the physical description of the robust von Kramm nor his manner. Rudolf was thoughtful and introspective, and therefore melancholic; perhaps the most Hamlet-like of the real princes. Rudolf's suicide in January, 1889, does not disqualify him as a candidate, but his whole character does.

3. **Archduke Franz Ferdinand.** A consumptive who single-mindedly overcame his affliction, he was perhaps the most determined of the later Hapsburgs. Imposing he was, but not flamboyant. After marrying a lady-in-waiting morganatically, he lived happily ever after in unusual archducal domestic bliss, or at least until that June Sunday in Sarajevo. Franz Ferdinand was entirely too stiff and bristly to have been the original von Kramm.

4. **Kaiser Wilhelm II.** While the absence of any reference to his imperious moustaches and withered left arm is suggestive, for a reference to either would have been a dead give-away, he was only of average height and size. Like his friend Franz Ferdinand, he was the very

model of a bourgeois family man; moreover, he took his role as First Bishop of the Lutheran Church with ponderous Germanic seriousness. He did have some rather mauve close companions, such as Count Eulenberg, but like the Scotch verdict, nothing untoward was ever proved. La Belle Otero did claim to have had an affair on the yacht *Hohenzollern* in the spring of 1901, but it is also not proved.

5. **Edward VII, as Prince of Wales.** Certainly this candidate had his share of affairs of the heart, as the French so euphemistically and illogically phrase it, and he did possess a profound Germanic accent; but while wide (he was called Tum-Tum by the irreverent), he was not tall. Like von Kramm, he could be obtuse, but the opulent oriental garb easily bars the Prince of Wales as a fit candidate. Albert Edward was scrupulous, indeed meticulous in his dress, and most English. He who popularized the homburg would never stoop to the astrakhan.

6. **King Milan Obrenovitch IV.** Although described as "a young, rich, handsome prince, gallant in bearing," and apparently the inspiration for Prince Danilo in *The Merry Widow*, this king of Serbia may be quickly dismissed as a possibility, as he lacked the requisite Germanic quarterings, and since the only language which he spoke until he was 14 was a Roumanian dialect,[9] there would have been no German accent.

7. **Prince Alexander Battenburg.** The first prince of Bulgaria at age 22, he was German, and a dashing figure. Michael Harrison makes a most convincing case for him. Alexander and Queen Victoria's granddaughter, the daughter of Victoria the Princess Royal of Germany, fell in love in 1884; but it was an ill-starred romance, and Alexander was obliged to renounce her in 1885 by Emperor Wilhelm I of Germany. The next year he was obliged by the Russians to renounce his throne, and in 1889 he married an Austrian actress. If dates are significant, the *Scandal in Bohemia* would have to be moved

40

up to 1884, which is not insupportable except to chronologists; but more significantly, Alexander, while tall, was slight, and does not meet the psychological portrait painted by Watson.

Who then was the masked man? Was there ever a prototype, and if so, can he be identified across the abyss of the intervening years?

It is submitted that the search requires a particular approach; that is, a psychological analysis in addition to the historical approach; but the search does lead directly to Ferdinand of Saxe-Coburg-Gotha, the Second Prince and first Tsar of Bulgaria.

The interpretation of Nigel Bruce notwithstanding, John Watson was both subtle and shrewd, and probably deliberately portrayed himself as being rather obtuse as a counterpoint to Holmes. Bruce's Watson could never have recorded the Holmes adventures; no Boobus Britannicus would have been capable of following the close reasoning of Holmes nor of being able to include all of the empirical data necessary to construct the Holmesian syllogism. We know Watson juggled dates and names, whether place or proper, but there was never any infidelity as to character. His psychological portraits were superb, and when he limned a person, that person remained properly defined as an individual.

As clothing connotes character, it is a good point at which to commence an examination of Watson's King of Bohemia. The king's "barbaric opulence" is amply documented by the references to the slashed astrakhan on his coat, the flame-coloured silk lining of his cloak, the flaming beryl serving as a neck-brooch for the self-same cloak, the fur-topped boots and of course the emerald snake ring.

Prince Ferdinand of Bulgaria was an elaborate and excessive dresser, wearing clothing which sometimes approached the bizarre. One of the rather large group of royal ladies who declined to be his princess, Louisa, a daughter of the Grand Duke of Tuscany, described his garb when he proposed thusly: "Ferdinand was most elaborately attired in a light grey suit with an ultra-chic Panama hat. He constantly waved his well-manicured hands and displayed the costly rings which glittered on his fingers. He attitudinized like a Narcissus, and kept posing until he thought doubtless I was sufficiently impressed with his fine figure, his rings, and last but not least, his smart yellow boots."[10]

Not only did he enjoy rings and precious stones as well as fur-trimmed boots, but it is documented that on a formal visit to Paris his blue toque was "bordered with white Astrakhan fur."[11]

Of additional and related significance is the seemingly carelessly dropped reference to the thick pink-tinted notepaper. The color pink possesses profound pejorative implications far beyond color. References to pink, then as now, suggest social improprieties of the grosser sort; and indeed Ferdinand's cousin Queen Victoria characterized him as "effeminate,"[12] and the Grand Duchess Marie Pavlovna more delicately observed that he had "a complex personality and foibles."[13] He was, in short, a thoroughgoing sensualist; so much so that no single sex could apparently satisfy his appetites. A *viveur* and *flaneur*, he also demonstrated more than a cursory interest in blond, blue-eyed adjutants.

Watson limns a rather specific portrait of the Bohemian King.

8. He was a Germanophone with a significant Bohemian connection. Like the King, Ferdinand possessed the "strong-marked German accent" referenced by Watson, for after all, he was a German prince who lived in Vienna.

As for the Bohemian connection, of course the imperial capital of the Bohemian crown land, was Vienna; Ferdinand also had an estate at Murany in Slovakia, then a part of Hungary. Indeed, when Ferdinand travelled incognito, he did so as the Count of Murany.

1. He was wealthy. Holmes was perhaps too quick to observe that "there is money in the case," but Ferdinand was the possessor of great inherited wealth, thanks to a distinctly non-royal but very rich Hungarian grandmother.

2. He was an imposing figure. Watson's description is that he "could hardly have been less than six feet six inches, with the limbs and chest of a Hercules." Ferdinand was described as having a "tall, massive figure," as well as "a six-foot figure and wasp waist."[14]

3. He was a person of strong character. "A thick hanging lip and a long straight chin suggestive of resolution pushed to the lengths of obstinacy," was Watson's description. This author has found no pictures of Ferdinand without a moustache; but the lip does not appear to be either thick or hanging. As this does not appear to symbolize any character trait, it does not seem to be material; however, his early beardless photographs evidence a strong and resolute chin. Count von Burian, the shrewd Austrian minister to Bulgaria, observed that Ferdinand "vigorously seized the reins of government and has not allowed even for one moment that there should arise any doubt about his determination to occupy to the full the position which has been given…"[15]

4, Apparently he had no nose. Watson vouchsafes no particulars about what is certainly the most distinctive of the facial features. While arguably it was concealed under the black vizard mask worn by the Count in an effort to be undetected (rather than unobserved, one hopes), the fact is he did remove it upon Holmes' identification. The omission is significant: why would such an acute observer and meticulous chronicler as Watson not have mentioned it? It is submitted that faithfully to portray the nose would have made the real identity of the Count immediately recognizable to his contemporaries. Ferdinand possessed an extremely large and distinctive nose, one verging upon the appellation proboscis, and it was described by one writer as a "huge Bourbon nose, which surged out and curved downwards in a smooth arc,"[16] and by another somewhat more gently as a "sensitive, arrogant long nose."[17] Indeed, "he was self-conscious about his nose throughout his life. As God's gift to the political cartoonists for over 30 years, from his accession to the Bulgarian throne in 1887 to his fall in 1918, he was unlikely to forget about it."[18] So the significance of the omission is that the inclusion may quite have given the game away. To have mentioned it would have been *lèse majesté*, and to have avoided mentioning a part of the face routinely described is to emphasize it by exclusion, the greatest emphasis of all. So here is another of Watson's subtle but strong clues.

5. **Antecedents.** The King's proper names were clearly and defiantly German: Wilhelm Gottsreich Sigismond[19] von Ormstein, as was his ducal title, the Grand Duke of Cassel-Felstein, and even the royal title related to Bohemia, which was an Austrian crownland. His accent was Germanic, and he himself announced that he had come incognito from Prague. Ferdinand shared a Germanic ambience, being a Prince of the ducal House of Saxe-Coburg-Gotha, and living at the Coburg Palais in Vienna. The family estate of Murany was in the Hungarian province of Slovakia, which was formerly allied to Bohemia within the Republic of Czechoslovakia.

6. **Age.** Watson reported the King's age as being 30 at the time of the investigation, which has been variously dated as March 1888 by one chronologist and 1889 by four of that breed. Watson himself dated it as occurring in 1888, but whatever the correct date, it was certainly no later than some weeks prior to July 1891, which is the occurrence of its earliest publication. Prince Ferdinand was born February 26, 1861; so he would have been 30 years of age in 1891. And if Ferdinand be the original of the King of Bohemia, the maximum pressure would have occurred then because of his frantic search for a royal bride.

7. **The Problem.** The pressing problem which brought the King to Holmes was his prospective marriage to Clotilde Lothman von Saxe-Meiningen of the strict-principled royal house of Scandinavia. Although

purportedly Scandinavian, the princess possessed a Germanic patronymic evocative of Ferdinand's own patronymic of Saxe-Coburg-Gotha.

Like the Bohemian King, Ferdinand was assiduously seeking a royal consort. Stamboloff, his prime minister, had been urging the necessity for some time, all for the continuity of the fledgling dynasty. Bulgaria, that improbable principality created by the Congress of Berlin, remained a part of the Ottoman Empire and the sultan was the liege lord of the Prince of Bulgaria. Like every parvenu ruler, an established royal house was necessary, and particularly so when an alienated Russia was actively seeking Ferdinand's assassination. Indeed, the state itself was at hazard without a royal heir. Is it any wonder that von Kramm observed that the matter"...is of such weight it may have an influence upon European history?"

There was Ferdinand's unsuccessful pursuit of Louisa, the daughter of the Grand Duke of Tuscany in 1891, and the next year there was marital maneuvering at Balmoral regarding English royalty, resulting in an equally unsuccessful *dénouement.* Two Wittelsbach princesses were vetoed by Wilhelm II, but by January 1893 the indefatigable Ferdinand's engagement was announced to Marie-Louise, the eldest daughter of duke Robert of Bourbon-Parma, with the marriage occurring the following April.

8. The Candidate. While there is respectable authority for the claims of several of the candidates, it is submitted that the most persuasive possibility is Prince Ferdinand. He was the son of a non-reigning prince of the Grand Duchy of Saxe-Coburg-Gotha, the grandson of Louis Philippe, the last King of France, cousin of Queen Victoria and a relative, directly or indirectly, of most of Europe's rulers. His particular branch of the family owed its considerable wealth to a grandfather's marriage to a Hungarian grandmother, poor in quarterings but rich otherwise. The family lived in the imposing Coburg Palais in Vienna, which was the glittering first city of Europe until the First World War.

Ferdinand was a cavalry officer in the Austrian army, and his duties did not deny him the abundant opportunities for pleasure available to a rich young nobleman in 19th century Vienna. He was, in fact, known patronizingly as a *salon prinz*, the then-current disparaging equivalent of the earlier term "carpet knight." Although regarded as an absurd princeling, vain and pleasure-wasted, he was ambitious and either crafty or shrewd, depending upon whether you inquired from one of his many enemies or few friends. His guile stood him in good stead, however, in maneuvering an invitation from the Bulgarian Sobrainie to become the Second Prince of Bulgaria in 1887, later in elevating himself to Tsar in 1908, and in delicately balancing between Russia and Austria-Hungary between those two dates. He abdicated in 1918, thus saving the dynasty until 1944 when the old imperialism of the new Russia toppled the throne. Ferdinand himself not surprisingly survived, cosseted in comfortable circumstances in a family palace at Coburg, Germany, until his death in 1948.

Watson's superb psychological portraits rest upon their careful descriptions, and it is only the conventional data as to names, places, dates with which Watson dissembles so gratuitously. Ferdinand of Bulgaria fits the psychological portrait of the King of Bohemia like a glove; Irene Adler would have appealed to him, and he to her, for both were shrewd and daring, hazard possessed an undeniable appeal to each, and their response to life was equally flamboyant, unconventional, and yes, bohemian — another of those subtle Watsonian touches.

Ferdinand was quite right; Irene would have made a splendid consort, for she had both spirit and style. It was Sherlock who was in error, and who made one of his few mistakes in so seriously underestimating his client. Secretive Ferdinand would have been particularly pleased at Holmes's misprize of him, and one hopes that the July 1891 issue of *The Strand*, doubtlessly delivered in an official Bulgarian diplomatic pouch, was read by a delighted Ferdinand in the regal seclusion of one of his exotic palaces.

NOTES

1. Both tsar and king are cognate terms, both tracing their origin to Caesar.
2. William S. Baring-Gould, *The Annotated Sherlock Holmes*, Vol. 1, p. 353, Clarkson Potter, New York.
3. J. Finley Christ, *The Scandal Behind the Scandal*, SHJ 9, No. 3, 1969, pp. 82–85; Julian Wolff, *The Arms of the King of Bohemia*, BSJ, Vol. 15, No. 3 (N.S.) September, 1965, pp. 147–149.
4. T. S. Blakeney, *A Case for Identification — in Bohemia*, SHJ Vol. 3, No. 2 (Tenth Issue), Winter 1956, pp. 15–16.
5. John D. Clark, *The King of Bohemia*, BSJ, Vol. 15, No. 3 (N.S.), September, 1965, pp. 142–146.
6. Edgar W. Smith, *A Scandal in Identity*, Profile by Gaslight, p. 262, *et seq.*, Simon and Schuster, 1944.
7. Herbert Eaton, *The King of Bohemia Unmasked*, The Vermissa Herald, Vol. 3, No. 1, January 1969.
8. Julian Blackburn, *The Identity of the King of Bohemia*, BSJ, Vol. 21, No. 2 (N.S.) June 1971; E V. Girand, *On the Antiquity of Scandal in Bohemia*, BSJ Vol. 23, No. 3 (N.S.) September 1973; Michael Harrison, *Sherlock Holmes and the King of Bohemia, the Solution of Royal Mystery, Beyond Baker Street*, p. 137 *et seq.*, Bobbs-Merrill 1976.
9. Francis Gerard, *A King's Romance*, Hutchinson and Co., London 1903.
10. Stephen Constant, *Foxy Ferdinand, Tsar of Bulgaria*, Watts, New York, 1980, p. 132.
11. *Ibid*, p. 237.
12. *Ibid*, p. 36.
13. *Ibid*, p. 211.
14. *Ibid*, p. 37.
15. *Ibid*, p. 83.
16. *Ibid*, p. 37.
17. *Ibid*, p. 317.
18. *Ibid*, p. 37.
19. Watson's spelling of Sigismond is in the French fashion. German usage was Sigismund. Possibly this is another subtle Watsonian touch suggesting a soupcon of French ancestry.

The Queen

A QUEEN has always been a significant player in every fairy tale, but most often she was portrayed as evil, usually in the role of a stepmother.

Our Queen was not a stepmother, but the mother of several children, and perhaps not a good mother to all nor to any; but in addition she was the Mother of England. In balance, she was a better mother to England.

Our Queen is Victoria, born May 24, 1819 to Mary Louisa Victoria, the Duchess of Kent, the former widowed Princess of Leiningen, who was a member of the ducal house of Saxe-Coburg-Gotha. Victoria had a half-sister, Feodora, and a half-brother, Karl. Her father, the Duke of Kent, is chiefly remembered for providing an heir to the throne, and for then decently dying after he performed that particular and necessary duty.

Her mother was a full-blooded German and her father was also German-blooded, being of the House of Hanover. All three Hanoverian Georges were of German extraction, including the father of George III, who died as Prince of Wales, and each of their wives were also German. So it was that the bulk of Victoria's heritage was German, and, of course, she married a German. It was a strong heritage.

She was christened Alexandrina Victoria and originally called Drina, thus it was purely fortuitous that we are not writing about the Alexandrine age rather than the Victorian. Just as her age was well-documented, so was her life, for we have her *Journals*, kept faithfully and frankly throughout her long life. It is thanks to them that a biographer of Victoria can offer her own views on all sorts of matters, unvarnished and uninterpreted.

Victoria was married in 1840 to Albrecht, anglicized to Albert, a German cousin, after proposing to him, as befits a monarch. Their marriage was idyllic, not just after his death, but before. They worked together, at adjoining desks, and it was clearly his influence which gave her new senses of purpose, facility and strength, which she never lost, even after his early death in December, 1861. She wrote to her Uncle Leopold, the brother of her mother, and the King of Belgium, in February, 1861: "On Sunday we celebrated, with feelings of deep gratitude and love, the twenty-first anniversary of our blessed marriage, a day which had brought us, and I may say, the world at large, such incalculable blessings! Very few can say with me that their husband at the end of twenty-one years is not only full of the friendship, kindness, and affection which a truly happy marriage brings with it, but the same tender love of the very first days of our marriage!"[1] In her *Journal* entry for December 14th, 1899, in the midst of the Boer War, she remembered the anniversary of his death, observing: "Already thirty-eight years since that dreadful catastrophe which crushed and changed my life, and deprived me of my guardian angel, the best of husbands and most noble of men!"[2]

QUEEN VICTORIA

Unfortunately and inaccurately, she has entered history as a solemn and officious old lady without humor and without feelings. Her *Journals* and letters give the lie to these notional views. She was most effective in dealing with death. Her entry for October 21, 1875, records her visit to the mother of one of her favorite Scottish retainers, John Brown, following the death of her retainer's husband. "We took some whisky and water and cheese, according to the universal Highland custom, and then left, begging the dear old lady to bear up."[3] Four years later, on June 21, 1879, the occasion of the death of the French Prince Imperial, she wrote to her eldest daughter, and her confidante, "Your sore heart would bleed for the poor, poor Empress — who has lost her all, her only child and the only hope she had left. And in such a horrible way. Good, exemplary, brave but alas! far too daring young man, and to think of his being murdered in such a way — though I am sure it was the affair of a few seconds — is enough for ever to haunt a mother's heart."[4]

Injustice offended her. She wrote to Prime Minister Salisbury on September 9th, 1899, "I am too horrified for words at this monstrous horrible sentence against this poor martyr Dreyfus. If only Europe would express its horror and indignation."[5] Nor did she like religious cant, writing to her daughter, the Crown Princess of Prussia on June 16, 1867: "The only objection which I have to him (Prince Leopold's tutor) is that he is a clergyman. However he is enlightened and so free from the usual prejudices of his profession that I feel I must get over my dislike to that. Mr. Duckworth is an excellent preacher and good-looking besides."[6]

In another letter to the Crown Princess of Prussia, this one dated December 18, 1867, she observed: "I wished to answer what you said about the bar between high and low. What you said about it is most true (the lower classes must rise to the upper — and vice versa — or the consequences are dreadful, as the French Revolution has proved) but alas! that is the great danger in England now, and one which alarms all right-minded and thinking people. The higher classes — especially the aristocracy (with of course exceptions and Honourable ones) are so frivolous, pleasure-seeking, heartless, selfish, immoral and gambling that it makes one think of the days before the French Revolution. The young men are so ignorant, luxurious and self-indulgent — and the young women so fast, frivolous and imprudent that the danger really is very great, and they ought to be warned. The lower classes are becoming so well-informed, are so intelligent and earn their bread and riches so deservedly — they cannot and ought not to be kept back — to be abused by the wretched, ignorant, high-born beings who live only to kill time. They must be warned and frightened or some dreadful crash will take place. What I can, I do, and will do — but Bertie ought to set a good example in these respects by not countenancing even any of these horrid people."[7]

But Bertie, the Prince of Wales, was a tough customer to maneuver, and his mother, the Queen, knew him well. In a letter of July 29, 1863 to her daughter, the Crown Princess, she noted: "Poor Bertie! — he is very affectionate and dutiful but he is very trying. The idleness is the same — and there is a great roughness of manner to his brothers and sisters which must be got the better of. Still, he is most anxious to do what is right, that is every thing. But his idleness and *'desoeuvrement'*, his listlessness and want of attention are great, and cause me much anxiety."[8]

Distrusting his judgment, she was reluctant to permit him responsibility. In a letter to him on March 9, 1868 she observed: "I have heard from Mr. Disraeli on the subject of your going to Ireland, and, as the Government seem to wish it so much, and to think that it will do so much good, I will naturally sanction it. But I much regret that the occasion chosen should be 'races,' as it naturally strengthens the belief, already far too prevalent, that your chief object is amusement; and races have become so bad of late, and the connection with them has ruined so many young men, and broken the hearts thereby of so many fond and kind parents, that I am especially anxious you should not sanction or encourage them."[9] The Queen warned in vain, for the Prince's horses would win some of the most prestigious races, including the Derby.

While she did not offer him meaningful employment, which was certainly a mistake, but it didn't ultimately adversely effect his kingship, and she did care for him. In her *Journal* entry of November 9, 1889 she noted: "Dear Bertie's 42nd birthday. may God bless and long preserve him for the good of his country! Warm-hearted, kind, and amiable, he is always a very good son to me."[10]

She also had problems with one of her grandsons, later Kaiser Wilhelm II of Germany. As early as 1868 she wrote to his mother, the Crown Princess of Prussia: "What you told me of dear Willy interested me very much. I share your anxiety especially as regards pride and selfishness. In our days — when a Prince an only maintain his position by his character — pride is most dangerous. And then besides I do feel strongly that we are before God all alike, and that in the twinkling of an eye, the highest may find themselves at the feet of the poorest and lowest. I have seen the noblest, most refined, high-bred feelings in the humblest and most unlearned, and it is most necessary a Prince should feel."[11] After he was Emperor, he insisted on being addressed in private as 'his Imperial Majesty.' She characterized it in a letter to Lord Salisbury, the Prime Minister, as "perfect madness," warning that "if he has such notions he (had) better never come here. The Queen will not swallow this affront."[12] When Wilhelm was forty, she noted in her *Journal*, without any grandmotherly feelings "I wish he were more prudent and less impulsive at such an age!"[13]

The Queen spent most of her time working — "doing her boxes" as she put it — studying the documents and reports sent to her by the Prime Minister. Walter Bagehot, in his seminal work *The English Constitution*, observed that the Crown had the rights to be consulted, to encourage and to warn, all of which rights the Queen regarded as responsibilities and performed throughout the longest reign in English history.

Like many tiny women, she had sinews of steel, giving full and free rein to her views, which she shared, sometimes unremittingly, with her premiers. Here was a message to Lord Beaconsfield, the former Benjamin Disraeli, dated June 27, 1877: "The Queen must write to Lord Beaconsfield again and with the greatest earnestness on the very critical state of affairs. From so many does she hear of the great anxiety evinced that the Government should take a firm, bold line. This delay — this uncertainty, by which, abroad, we are losing our prestige and our position, while Russia is advancing and will be before Constantinople in no time! Then the Government will be fearfully blamed and the Queen so humiliated that she thinks she would abdicate at once. Be bold!"[14]

She directed the following message to her private secretary, Sir Henry Ponsonby, on September 17, 1882 regarding one of England's many border wars: "The Queen does not like the words 'early withdrawal of troops' and would wish Sir Henry to cypher as follows: The Queen to Earl Granville — Think you should be very cautious in speaking of early withdrawal of troops. We must bind ourselves to nothing. We have not fought and shed precious blood and gone to great expense for nothing."[15]

And this to Prime Minister William Ewart Gladstone, whom she never liked, complaining that he talked to as if she was a public meeting: "6 May 1886. The Queen is anxious, before leaving for Windsor, to repeat to Mr. Gladstone what she tried to express — but which she thinks perhaps she did not do very clearly — viz.: that her silence on the momentous Irish measures, which he thinks it is his duty to bring forward, does not imply her approval, or acquiescence in them. The Queen writes this with pain, as she always wishes to be able to give her Prime Minister her full support, but it is impossible for her to do so, when the union of the Empire is in danger of disintegration and serious disturbance."[16]

There was a quality of plain speaking about her, which remains refreshing today, particularly for a ruler. Here was a message to Lord Salisbury on July 9, 1889: "I am quite horrified to see the name of that horrible lying

Labouchere and of that rebel Parnell on the Committee for the Royal Grants. I protest vehemently against both. It is quite indecent to have such people on such a Committee."[17]

This frank quality was not limited to governmental matters. Here is a letter of October 21, 1874 to Theodore Martin: "What does Mr. Martin say to the dreadful indiscretion and disgracefully bad taste of Mr. Reeve in publishing Mr. C. Granville's scurrilous Journal, without eliminating what is very offensive and most disloyal towards the Sovereigns he served, and the Sovereigns and Princes whose hospitality and even intimacy he enjoyed! And to leave the names in full when the children and near relatives of those he abuses are alive, is unheard of! The Queen hopes and wishes Mr. Reeve will and should know what she thinks of such conduct. It is especially revolting to her, as she is put in comparison with her uncle and predecessors who, though undignified and peculiar and not highly gifted, was (sic) very honest, most extremely conscientious and anxious to do his (sic) duty, and most kind to herself, though not always in a judicious manner. The Queen is determined that on some occasion or other she will make known what she knows of his character. Of George IV he speaks in such shocking language; language not fit for any gentleman to use of any other gentleman or human being, still less of his Sovereign."[18] Powerful stuff that.

She was no fool. After a riot at Trafalgar Square, she distinguished between the "deserving unemployed" and "the horrid thieves and a few socialists."[19]

Her interests went beyond her royal duties. She interested herself even in the Whitechapel murders. In addition to writing to the Home Secretary with four most specific and practical suggestions as to locating the murderer, she wrote to the Lord Salisbury, the then Prime Minister, on November 10, 1888: "This new most ghastly murder shows the absolute necessity for some very decided actions. All these courts must be lit, and our detectives improved. They are not what they should be.

You promised, when the first murder took place, to consult with your colleagues about it."[20]

She was fearless. When Lincoln was assassinated, she observed in her *Journal* that she trusted it would not be catching. There were attempts on her life, and in 1867 she wrote to her daughter, the Crown Princess of Prussia, from Balmoral: "Gen. Grey asked to see me when I came in, and said he was sorry to alarm me, but must show me the telegram...reporting...the news from a reliable source, that the Fenians had said they meant to try and seize me here and were starting today or tomorrow! Too foolish."[21]

Victoria had another quality which was unusual in a queen; which was an essential modesty. The Duchess of Buccleuch once told her that she had not asked to be introduced to Cecil Rhodes because she understood he disliked women and was rude to them. The Queen was surprised, observing that "I don't think that can be so, because he was very civil to me when he came here."[22]

The most appropriate analysis of her role was stated by the author of her biography in the *Encyclopedia Britannica*,"None will question her high sense of duty as wife, mother and queen, or the transparent honesty, the massive simplicity of her royal character."[23]

She died at her beloved Osborne, rich in years and honors, in 1901, and her death ended not only the century, but also the Victorian age, which due to her dominance, assumed her name. Some lady. Some Queen.

NOTES

1. Page 153, Hibbert, Christopher, editor, *Queen Victoria in her Letters and Her Journals*, Viking, New York, 1985
2. Page 341, *Ibid.*
3. Page 241, *Ibid.*
4. Page 258, *Ibid.*
5. Page 339, *Ibid.*
6. Page 197, *Ibid.*

7. Page 199, *Ibid.*
8. Page 166, *Ibid.*
9. Page 204, *Ibid.*
10. Page 283, *Ibid.*
11. Page 205, *Ibid.*
12. Page 313, *Ibid.*
13. Page 337, *Ibid.*
14. Page 245, *Ibid.*
15. Page 276, *Ibid.*
16. Page 298, *Ibid.*
17. Page 316, *Ibid.*
18. Page 238, *Ibid.*
19. Page 297, *Ibid.*
20. Page 314, *Ibid.*
21. Page 200, *Ibid.*
22. Page 31, Ponsonby, Sir Frederick, *Recollections of Three Reigns*, Eyre & Spottiswoode, London, 1951
23. Page 130, Volume 23, Chicago, 1966

The Judge

NEVER WAS there a medieval morality play, nor seldom a melodrama, which was its nineteenth century stage permutation, without a judge, sometimes so acting but not always so designated. The Canon cannot, in candid retrospect, be excluded from that lineage or those properties forming the qualities of such productions

From our particular perch atop the end of the twentieth and the beginning of the twenty first centuries, we tend to be parochial about such productions, but they were good theater and performed the function of teaching people who did not read at all or seldom. They are good drama, as is the Canon, and for that reason alone, they are worth considering within the aegis of an art form.

JOHN FRANCIS MORIARTY

Our judge was not one from within the confines of the Canon, but one which antedated it and furnished a genesis for a strong character — Professor Moriarty. He was represented as evil incarnate, and his antecedent was a fellow student of Arthur Conan Doyle at Stonyhurst.

The lad was an Irishman, then a constituent part of the United Kingdom, and his name was John Francis Moriarty. He became a high court judge, and as an adult, at least, demonstrated no traits which form the utterly evil character of the professor, although he did possess traits which were keenly unattractive and which would have been grossly offensive to Doyle. According to Father Turner, S.J., the resident archivist at Stonyhurst, Doyle had determined that his religious development did not permit him to take communion, and so he did not, which could be troublesome in a Roman Catholic school staffed and run by Jesuits. His declination showed great credit to Doyle, and this marked ethical attitude persisted throughout his entire life. Now, according to Father Turner, while young John Francis Moriarty privately ridiculed religion, in public he was most devout, ostentatiously taking communion. Moriarty never ceased to be pious in public; a wise but disreputable course as he returned to Ireland, where piety was a given for preferment.

Fr. Turner furnished me with a copy of the obituary of Moriarty from *The Stonyhurst Magazine*. He died during the first years of what was then called the Great War, but his death had nothing to do with the war, being consequent to an operation. It was clear from the obituary that he had been a barrister, which led to successive appointments to the office of Solicitor General and Attorney General for Ireland, and ultimately to the Irish Bench as a Lord Justice of Appeal.

There were other obituaries, of course, as he died a member of the highest court in Ireland, but obituaries are the least reliable reporters, for the subject is recently dead, and there is good and sufficient authority that one does not speak ill of the dead. Indeed, this folk injunction was first heard over two thousand years ago in Rome, and it was then sufficiently ancient that it became an aphorism — *de mortius nil nisi bonum*.

The obituary in the *Dublin Express* reported that "He was admitted to the Irish Bar in 1877. A few years afterwards he had built up a large and growing practice as a junior. Following his first marriage, he retired from the Bar for several years. Soon after his return he rapidly came into prominence, appearing as a junior in several famous cases. He took silk[1] in 1904, and thereafter his rise to fame was meteoric. In practically every case of note he was amongst the leading counsel on one side or the other. His legal skill, great as it was, seemed to be dwarfed by his forceful and silver-tongued oratory."

The obituary in the *Irish Times* was a bit more enthusiastic. "Lord Justice Moriarty was a man of learning and culture, whilst his accurate and intimate knowledge of men and public affairs was of the greatest possible assistance to him, both as a lawyer and a judge. Though he could be bitingly sarcastic when occasion required, he had a very kindly disposition, was a sincere friend, and would suffer much personal inconvenience to do an act of benevolence or charity."

The Irish Law Times limned his legal career, concluding as to the man: "The late Lord Justice was a man of great culture and wide reading, his knowledge of French literature being particularly extensive. In the library of the Four Courts, and indeed amongst the profession generally, his genial disposition and friendly nature gave him a right place in the affections of his brethren. He was one of the most kindly of men, and when he was at the Bar his charm of manner and his disposition made him exceedingly popular with all of who came in contact with him. Both the Bench and Bar deeply deplore his tragic death."

As is still customary in legal circles, when a lawyer or judge dies, the brethren gather and each who wishes recounts some experience with the decedent and may also relate what kind of a person he was, provided either honesty or kindness permits it. The Lord Chancellor of Ireland spoke similarly about his colleague, Moriarty, including the following observations: "The Lord Justice had a very hard fight in this life — a curious fight — and he fought it with courage with energy, and with consummate ability. Out of his weakness he made himself strong, and in the end he obtained the fruition of what he was looking for. The terrible tragedy which they all felt was that the man who fought this great fight, and fought it so well, should, at the moment of its fruition, and seeing himself put where he was in no way unworthy of the great names that had gone before him, should at that moment be struck down." We can only speculate as to what constituted that hard and curious fight. As drink has always been regarded as the Irish curse, that would be an easy assay as the reason, but that would hardly fit as the Lord Chancellor referred to the fight as curious, which is not the adjective which an Irishman would use with respect to liquor.

Moriarty died May 2nd, 1915, in Birmingham, England, after surgery for an illness that was sudden but undisclosed. His estate was not large, amounting to only 12,486 pounds sterling. His furniture and library were sold at auction, and among the books sold was a fifty year run of *Punch* from 1841 to 1891. If *The Strand* was also among his effects, it is not reported. And if it was, did the real identity of the evil professor register with him? I am certain that it did.

He was born in 1853 or 1855 in Mallow, in the county of Cork, the son of a solicitor and large landowner. He was educated at Stonyhurst, where he came in contact with Doyle, and later at Trinity University in Dublin, where he studied law.

As a barrister, he lived in Dublin, but like most advocates, travelled on a circuit, in his case, the Munster Circuit, located in Southern Ireland, and which area included his boyhood home of Mallow. He lived at 125, Lower Baggot Street, and later at 40, Lower Leeson Street, later at 92, Lower Leeson Street, and finally at 47, Stephen's Green, all in Dublin. It was a progression of increasing affluence.

He married two widows, first Katherine Kavanaugh, who resided at 20 Merrion Square in Dublin, in July 1883, and in 1909, Mabel Agnes, daughter of Henry de Blaquiere, of Fiddan House, County Galway, and the widow of Hubert Peter Dophin, of Turoe, in the same county. Neither wife survived him but both brought money to their marriages. The funeral notice listed as survivors, three daughters, Marguerite, Joan (Frances Caroline) and Nell O'Reilly, but these were stepdaughters.

John Moriarty, the father of John Francis Moriarty, had two other sons who were connected with the law: Michael A. Moriarty, a solicitor, and James Moriarty, a barrister resident in Sydney, New South Wales, who was the eldest son and his father's heir.

I have been quite unable to locate any of the Moriarty papers. Ms. Pamela Bradley, the able Irish researcher I was fortunate to have retained, was at a dinner party with a Queen's Counsel from Northern Ireland recently, and broached the subject of Moriarty. He knew of his reputation and observed that he thought Moriarty would have been careful not to leave any papers.

So it was quickly apparent that Moriarty was a devious man with secrets, and someone not unlike the persona of the professor. Like Holmes, he manifestly desired no biographer.

There is presently a Moriarty who is on the high Irish Court. He disclaims any relationship with the earlier judge, and was at some pains to limn his own ancestry to give credence to that nonrelationship. He suggested that the record to examine was *The Old Munster Circuit*, by Maurice Healy, in which he who was known as Johnny Moriarty had more than one entry, and thusfar it is the only known source of personal information about him. What now follows are quotations and references from that source.

"Johnnie Moriarty, as everybody called him, was called to the Irish Bar in 1877. He was born in Mallow, where his father practiced as a solicitor; Dick Hennessey used often to tell in his presence the pleasant legend that his grandfather had been a highwayman in command of two gangs of robbers, one of which operated between Mallow and Charleville, and the other between Mallow and Kanturk. Any trouble with the first band was promptly suppressed by punitive measures undertaken by the second and *vice versa*; the result was a steady and lucrative business which enabled the chief not merely to article his son to an attorney but also to give him a good grounding in the principles on which he should conduct his business! Johnnie always smiled when this tale was told, and I do not suppose that anybody paid much attention to Dick's pleasant malice."[2]

Healy, who also practiced on the Munster circuit, regarded John Francis Moriarty as "one of the most remarkable and one of the most unscrupulous advocates that ever practiced at the Irish Bar."[3] He recalled him making "the most powerful and eloquent speeches, using all the arts of the oratory choosing his words with literary judgment, and adorning his delivery with simple but graceful gestures. He was one of the best cross-examiners I ever knew; and he always knew when to leave well enough alone.... He had a magnetic personality, and the smile on his handsome face seemed to destroy the confidence of the witness opposed to him. I know of no advocate who ever defended prisoners with greater judgment or greater skill; when he prosecuted he was fair, but deadly. If it had not been for his cynicism and opportunism, I think he would have had more of my heart than any other of my brethren on the Circuit; and nobody has grieved more over the last sad chapters of a life that appeared to be destined to such great things."[4]

Mallow had been a safe parliamentary seat for the Liberals, but in 1883 William O'Brien, a native, returned there to run. He was a nationalist, a very fine journalist and a fiery speaker with an even more fiery message of an independent Ireland. The Liberal candidate was regarded as the winner until Moriarty entered as a Moderate, which could split the vote. The Liberals bought off Moriarty, who withdrew, although it was claimed he directed his supporters to O'Brien, who won the election. If he had so swung his supporters the Liberals never learned of it, for in a short period of time he was appointed by the Liberal government Crown Prosecutor for the Munster Circuit. Thereafter he became a Conservative and obtained a better appointment.[5]

In the early 1880's he married his first wife, who was

both widowed and wealthy. "The newly married couple both liked good living and sport; they frequented all the leading race-meetings and backed their fancies freely, with the usual consequences."[6] She died in 1898.

In the early 1890's he made a bet with a turf accountant, unfortunately named Silke, and won five hundred pounds, but an objection as to the winner was made. Moriarty convinced Silke to pay him at the race track but with the condition that the check would not be deposited until the objection had been ruled upon. Moriarty immediately deposited the check and sent out checks to other creditors against the deposited check. The Moriarty horse was determined to have lost and suit was brought by Silke against the bank, which tells a good deal about Moriarty and his assets.[7] Indeed, at one point Moriarty was obliged to declare himself a bankrupt, and at his public examination he was confronted by a creditor with a bill of over one hundred pounds for merchandise obtained by Moriarty. The small creditor claimed he would be ruined if he was not paid and the presiding judge turned to Moriarty and inquired if he could not offer something for the poor soul. "Moriarty pulled out of his pocket a handsome cigarcase and said: 'I can offer him a cigar!'"[8] The judge later recounted that he regretted that he did not than and there commit Moriarty for contempt.

In 1910 when the Nationalists were the majority party in Ireland he became a Nationalist. As Healy observed, "Moriarty promptly burgeoned forth as a full-blown Nationalist, but it was obvious that he was only seeking promotion. He was at length appointed Solicitor-General and after a short interval he became Attorney-General. He held that office during the most difficult period of Irish pre-war politics, and no man could utter a word of criticism of the way he discharged the duties of his office. He had to deal with the Dublin Strike, with the beginning of the trouble about the Volunteers, and with a number of other ticklish situations. He put an end to an old agrarian war in Kerry; and he achieved the paradox of keeping Ireland in the most peaceful and law-abiding state ever attained during the history of the Union, at a moment when three different organizations were drilling and arming to slaughter one another. At length he was appointed a Lord Justice of Appeal; but he only survived his appointment by a couple of years. He died in 1915;[9] and rumor has it that his last remark was "What won the 3:30?'"[10]

Whatever his considerable legal abilities, and they were great, so also was his lack of integrity. "Moriarty was an advocate of amazing ability. Tall and powerfully built, he made full use of his height when dominating a witness. To see him slowly rise like a great snake uncoiling was calculated to make the stoutest witness quail; and as he screwed in his monocle he seemed to be capable of looking into the innermost secrets of your heart. He had a number of mannerisms, amongst them an uncomfortable, mocking laugh, with which he pleasantly led a witness along the path to a trap, only to fly at him as soon as he was in the toils…Johnnie…was entirely unscrupulous in his conduct of a case…And when Johnnie purported to read from a document when he was cross-examining a witness, it was always prudent to call for the document and make sure that it was being accurately read. Johnnie loved a *finesse*, and was not very particular if it was permissible or not. He seemed to me to prefer to lose a case by a trick than win it by fair means."[11]

He, as Doyle observed when they were students at Stonyhurst, was not religious, but assumed religiosity when it served his purposes. He was not a practicing Catholic, nor a practicing anything, but he would publicly proclaim his Catholicism on those occasions when it was helpful. Once, during his opening statement, when the Angelus bell was heard, several jurors crossed themselves, so Moriarty did so also and bowed his head as if in prayer. Healy opined that Moriarty hadn't prayed the Angelus in forty years.[12] His equally irreligious opposing barrister did the same thing the following day, however, "so to even matters out," he explained.[13]

Healy recalled representing Mrs. Flurry O'Donoghue, the owner of a Killarney hotel, who had been involved in an accident from which a law action resulted. Moriarty represented the defendant. "In the course of her story Mrs. O'Donoghue happened to describe her little hotel with some satisfaction and pardonable complacency. Johnnie unwound himself with a sinister smile. 'So you live in this earthly paradise?' he asked. 'A regular Garden of Eden — tell me, have you any serpent there?'

'No Serjeant,[14] but we'd always be happy to see you!' replied the lady, bringing the cross-examination to an immediate and ignominious conclusion."[15]

Moriarty lived during the last days of the British raj in Ireland. It was a poor country dominated in every aspect by the English, and those of character on both sides of the Irish Sea regretted the systematic rapine of the land and its people. To this day the Irish retain an abiding hatred for the English, and Moriarty and others who allied themselves with the conquerors, are held in utter contempt. Then and now, the Irish are accomplished and zestful haters. Of Irish extraction, Doyle's feeling was not dictated by this animus for Doyle was opposed to an independent Irish state. Had Doyle lived in Ireland instead of England he would undoubtedly had been the target of what can be regarded as traditional Irish animosity.

The picture of Moriarty which is reproduced here, originally appeared in a Cork newspaper after his 1915 death. Even the most cursory examination reveals an obviously compelling look about the man, even without the monocle. Remember how Holmes described Professor Moriarty in the *Final Problem*? "He is extremely tall and thin, his forehead domes out in a white curve, and his two eyes are deeply sunken in his head. He is clean-shaven, pale and ascetic looking. He peered at me with great curiosity in his puckered eyes." If Doyle was describing Moriarty the judge, be could not have been more accurate. Was it prescience? Or did he so carefully remember the schoolboy Moriarty?

On the basis of what I learned at Stonyhurst, I wrote in another book[16] "I knew something about John Francis Moriarty. He became a barrister, practiced his profession in Ireland, then all of it a part of the United Kingdom. He was not an honorable man and sought to gain favor as a trimmer and as a publicly professing Catholic. He was successful at both. Using his wiles, which were many and disreputable, he became a king's counsel and then a high court judge. Unfortunately, in the law, as elsewhere, preferment is too often visited upon the undeserving and the unworthy. Father Turner thought that Doyle had selected the surname for the professor because he did not like John Francis Moriarty."

What of the Professor's Binomial Theorem? Is there any data from Stonyhurst which might have suggested that to Doyle? There is indeed, for the Stonyhurst records establish that in 1873, while Doyle was still there, the second prize for mathematics, some ten pounds, then a very substantial sum, was awarded to John Francis Moriarty.

What interaction between Doyle and Moriarty caused Doyle to make him an arch villain has never been fully known, and so long as the Doyle papers remain protected from the public, some sixty-seven years after his death, will certainly remain unknown.

But we do know that the student Moriarty undoubtedly furnished the surname for the evil professor, and if he did not supply the complete bill of particulars, he came close in his defiance of the laws of society, and he did, as Father Turner opined, create an enmity with Doyle, which undoubtedly arose from a monumental lack of Moriarty integrity.

Clearly and demonstrably, it was the Judge Moriarty who, in truth and in fact, was the Professor Moriarty of evil memory.

NOTES

1. Meaning that he was appointed a Kings Counsel, abbreviated as K.C., which is the ultimate professional accolade for an English barrister. The reference to silk was that the advocate now was permitted to wear a silk gown.
2. *The Old Munster Circuit*, by Maurice, Healy, 1939, page 85.
3. Page 84.
4. Page 84.
5. Page 86, 87.
6. Page 87.
7. The case is in the Irish Reports as National Bank v. Silke.
8. Page 88.
9. Actually, in 1915.
10. Pages 89, 90.
11. Page 93.
12. Page 92.
13. Page 92.
14. Moriarty was a serjeant at law, an honorary but significant legal position. When I was in Law School one of the professors asked for the name of any English serjeant at law. There was a long silence before someone, still unidentified, offered "Sergeant York."
15. Page 93.
16. Pages 37 to 39, *The Worth of the Game*, Gasogene Press Ltd., Dubuque, 1993.

The Villain

If the name of the villain, Moriarty, was furnished by a schoolmate at Stonyhurst, the Jesuit school which Doyle attended, the basic constituents of the villain were furnished by another Victorian, Mr. Adam Worth. The ultimate proof of this lies in the fact that Worth was known as the Napoleon of Crime, which was the professor's designation by Holmes himself.

In the *Encyclopedia of World Crime*, the author, Jay Robert Nash, writes, almost lovingly, of Adam Worth, which is not surprising, for Robert Pinkerton, his ancient adversary, felt the same way about him. Nash wrote at page 3188:

> "Adam Worth was beyond a doubt the greatest criminal mastermind of the nineteenth century. Sir Robert Anderson, chief of the Criminal Investigation Division at Scotland Yard, said of him 'he was the Napoleon of the criminal world. None other could hold a candle to him.' Allan Pinkerton, founder of the famed Pinkerton Detective Agency in the U.S., echoed this grudging respect, suggesting 'he was the Napoleon of crime, the greatest mastermind of them all.' These words were not lost on British author Arthur Conan Doyle, creator of Sherlock Holmes. In creating a criminal mind that would match his super-sleuth, Doyle patterned the cunning Professor James Moriarty after Adam Worth. At one point, Holmes tells his loyal associate: 'He is the Napoleon of crime, Watson. He is the organizer of half that is evil and nearly all that is undetected in this great city. He is a genius, a philosopher, an abstract thinker. He has a brain of the first order. He sits motionless, like a spider in the center of its web, but that web has a thousand radiations, and he knows well every quiver of each of them.'"

Ben Macintyre, who wrote a recent biography about

Worth, had as his thesis that he was "the real Moriarty." He quotes Vincent Starrett as identifying Worth as Moriarty, and Macintyre submits an ingenious proof that Moriarty's painting *La Jeune Fille a l'Agneau* was a Doylean play on the gallery Agnew, from which place the *Duchess of Devonshire* was stolen by Worth."

ADAM WORTH

Macintyre continued: "The Moriarty Doyle created had much in common with his role model. Like the devastatingly clever professor, Worth headed and directed an enormous international network of thieves, planning thefts no other in his day would dare commit, and traveling about the globe while living in splendor in the finest hotels or on the high seas aboard his private yacht. He, like Moriarty, enjoyed Oriental decor and the mysticism of the Far East. Also, like the professor, Worth confounded the efforts of the police of police on three continents, evading arrest and escaping prison, except in two instances."

Richard Wilmer Rowan, in his *The Pinkertons, A Detective Dynasty*, stated: "Worth was called, perhaps whimsically, the 'emperor of the underworld,' but he was also known to four continents as 'Little Adam,' and no criminal of modern times has ever had so many respectful things said about him by baffled police administrators. McClure Stevens in *Famous Crimes and Criminals*, quotes Sir Robert Anderson, who became chiedf of the Criminal Investigation Department at Scotland Yard while Adam Worth was at the height of his career, as having said of him: 'He was the Napoleon of the criminal world. None other could hold a candle to him.' Dapper, cultivated, well-dressed and affable, Adam, unlike most other New York criminals of his generation, abhorred the idea of employing force. Rarely did he permit himself a weapon of any sort, even when leading some strikingly desperate enterprise. He had a keen mind and a quick wit."[1]

Worth was born in 1844, but as with many things about his life, there are disputes: Nash places his birthplace in New York City of Jewish parents, and James D. Horan, author of *The Pinkertons. The Detective Dynasty That Made History*, claimed it was Cambridge, Massachusetts, while Macintyre asserted a German birth, relying in part on Worth's examination in his Belgian trial where he stated he arrived in the United States when he was five or six years of age. One is tempted to concluded that the weight of the evidence is that his parents were probably German Jews and he was either born in Germany or in America after his parents emigration.

Horan described him thusly, "Physically he was a slight man, five foot seven inches, and he never weighed more than 130 pounds. He had a sad, almost melancholy face, with large luminous dark eyes, thick black hair and luxurious sideburns that gave him a distinguished professorial appearance. He usually wore a frock coat, a gold watch chain, and a solitary pearl stickpin. He was vain about his appearance, and in his last days darkened his bushy eyebrows."[2]

If, as is generally believed, that Doyle drew on Worth for the type of man who was Moriarty, he did not choose to borrow his physical characteristics. In *The Final Problem*, Holmes describes Moriarty as"...extremely tall and thin, his forehead domes out in a wide curve, and his two eyes are deeply sunken in his head. He is clean-shaven, pale, and ascetic-looking, retaining something of the professor in his features. His shoulders are rounded from much study, and his face protrudes forward and is forever oscillating from side to side in a curiously reptilian fashion. He peered at me with great curiosity in his puckered eyes."

What is interesting is the reference by Holmes to "something of a professor" and Horan's reference to Worth as having "a distinguished professorial appearance." This reference is significantly confirmatory of the relationship between Worth and Moriarty. Indeed, I believe that the connection has been established, so that we may accept it as a verity.

What do we know about Worth? Both because his activities were criminal *and* successful, we know less than wish, however the sweep of his brush was so great in both America and Europe there are data, and the fact that Doyle knew of him evidences that Worth was not as unknown as Moriarty. Worth's first known crime was unsuccessful; sufficiently so that he was imprisoned at SingSing for a failed theft of a package from an Adams Express Company truck shortly after the Civil War.[3] If the crime was unsuccessful, his early escape from SingSing — by cunning rather than violence — was successful. It was the only crime for which he was ever convicted in the United States, which testifies to his intelligence and acumen. He was a very bright fellow, and his specialty was to plan the criminal activities which his minions performed. Sometimes he would participate in a given criminal caper, observing that he "wished to keep his hand in." And a clever hand it was, manifestly successful, and permitting him to live in whatever city he found himself, well and luxuriously.

Worth, dressed as a police constable, convinced a night watchman at an insurance company in Cambridge, Massachusetts, that a robbery was imminent, and was permitted access to the building. He had learned about explosives in prison and when the night watchman was in another part of the building, he blew the safe, obtaining some $30,000, the equivalent of more than $1,000,000 in today's dollars.

Worth then studied the Boylston National Bank of Boston, and developed a plan for robbing it. He rented space next to the bank, opened a store in the front half for the sale of wine bitters, and used the back half to tunnel into the bank, an arrangement not dissimilar to the enterprise of Mr. John Clay in *The Adventure of the Redheaded League*. He and Charles Bullard, the criminal son of a wealthy father, formed a partnership which lasted for some years. Both were men who enjoyed the good life, which was good food, good talk, good wine and bad women. Both had an identical interest in cultural matters which was absent from their colleagues in matters criminal.

In the evening of November 20, 1869 they, with the

help of their confederates, broke into the bank; Worth blew open the doors to the bank vault and they decamped with cash and negotiable securities in an amount equivalent today of several million dollars. The robbery was a *cause celebre*, complete with Pinkerton's being retained to find the criminals and the loot, so Worth and Bullard sailed to Liverpool, staying in elegant quarters. There they met Miss Kitty Flynn, a seventeen year old young woman, who was born in Ireland, and who has been characterized variously as a singer, waitress and a bartender. She was a beauty, and although both men loved her, she married Bullard, with Worth as the best man. Tradition asserts that Worth and Bullard shared Kitty's favors in a form of *menage-a-trois*. In matters of this sort hard evidence is difficult to come by, but at the least it can be confidently asserted that Kitty was, on occasion, generous of her person to each of them. She was, in the parlance of the time, a high stepper. Macintyre insists that the two daughters born during her marriage to Bullard were sired by Worth.

The Bullards, now renamed the Wells, moved to Paris, to which Worth (now called Henry J. Raymond, after the then owner and publisher of *The New York Times*) moved shortly thereafter. Wells and Worth, at the latter's instance, each invested substantial sums (believed to have been $75,000 each) into an elaborate cafe, bar, club and gambling establishment at 2, rue Scribe, which if my long-term memory is accurate is the site of the Grand Hotel Intercontinental. It was elegantly furnished and one of the Pinkertons claimed the faro gaming room was the most luxurious in Europe. Kitty was the hostess and her beauty ensnared many legitimate customers, as well as the criminal element which flocked to the establishment.

While the owners were regarded as legitimate businessmen, the business attracted the top crop of international criminals, for whom Worth provided, for a cut, all sorts of nefarious schemes, among which was forgery plan which cost the Bank of England an immense sum. Those who carried his criminal banner in this particular enterprise, as well as others, were Max Shinburn, Walter Sheridan, George McDonald, Austin Bidwell and George Bidwell. It is an interesting nuance that Doyle used the name of Sir George Burnwell in the *Adventure of the Beryl Coronet* to represent a thoroughly unscrupulous crook, which is very close to George Bidwell, who was, in truth and in fact, a thoroughly unscrupulous crook. Clearly, Doyle had at least a passing knowledge of criminal activities.

Worth is reported to have planned everything from frauds to burglaries to robberies in Turkey, the Netherlands, France, England, Germany and Belgium. He became extremely rich from his cuts on the criminal activities of his followers, and acquired a yacht, christened the Shamrock, which was named by Kitty Bullard. Parenthetically, it was believed contemporaneously that Worth was the father of Kitty Bullard's two daughters, and certainly it is true that Bullard disappeared for a time, during which Worth assisted her financially and emotionally.

During this time frame he acquired a prestigious London townhouse at 158, Piccadilly, but leading the bifurcated life which he chose, he also had a residence known as West Lodge, located on the west corner of Clapham Common. In addition, there was talk of a *pied-a-terre* in the slums of east London. The public persona, that is Henry J. Raymond, was a man who was a retired American businessman, distinguished and extremely well-dressed, a personage who dealt with important Englishmen and who enjoyed the many pleasures which wealth can bring. The private person, Adam Worth, was a slight man, known as "Little Adam," who dealt only with criminals who were either his confederates or his employees, and for whom he planned a myriad of criminal activities, all varied and invariably successful. It has been written "that a large part of Worth's criminal genius lay in his variety of plots. He could patiently tunnel through a building into a bank vault, or switch bags like a common confidence man, but he could also plan and carry out over long distances crimes that required an expert knowledge of larger commercial businesses and the minutiae of drafts, warehouse receipts, and supporting documents."[4]

One thing beyond success was a consistent practice with him. Worth denigrated force and violence. It was as unnecessary as it was dangerous. Those of his minions who used violence or carried weapons were unceremoniously drummed out of his organization, and were never reinvited. Brains, not brawn, was his forte. His criminal plans were not confined to one country or even one continent. He felt comfortable planning business even in the mideast — passing forged drafts in Symrna, now Izmir, then part of the Turkish Empire, but his henchmen failed him in their lack of precautions, were arrested and tried. Convicted, they languished in a Turkish prison, then and now the worst of prison systems. Worth went to Constantinople, where the prison was located, and using the beautiful wife of one of the imprisoned men, plus lavish bribes, obtained the necessary keys for copying. This copying of keys was one of his trademarks, which was used effectively in many circumstances, all of which resulted in substantial inroads on other people's property. He effected the surreptitious release of four out of the five men imprisoned, and returned with them to England.

If there is difficulty in reconstructing his professional life, which he went to great pains to keep murky for obvious reasons, there is even greater difficulty in investigating his personal life. There is considerable evidence that he maintained the *nom de plume* of Raymond for the balance of his life, subsequently marrying under that name and granting that name to two children born of that marriage to an American woman, she and they residing in Brooklyn, and he continuing his European occupations.

It has also been urged by one biographer[5] that he lived the life of an English country gentleman as Mr. Henry Elliott, owning an estate named Landale Manor, near Ottery St. Mary, in Devonshire. While rusticating there he became friendly with a neighbor, Major Anthony Waring, marrying his sister, Angela, and living contentedly and childlessly. It is claimed that while living there he was being blackmailed by Sophie Lyons of Detroit, an American confidence woman who fortuitously ran into him when he was in London with his wife, and that after paying her large sums for some period of time, he arranged with one Billy McCoy in Chicago to beat her up in an effort to discourage the blackmail, paying him twenty five thousand dollars in advance for that service. It is claimed that Miss Lyons died of her injuries occasioned by an attack in her home by a robber. The residence was placed at 676 Erie Boulevard in Detroit, and a date of the occurrence after June of 1899. Under this theory, he returned to his estate and lived contentedly under his vine and fig tree until his death there some years later. There is considerable specific data given in support of this theory, and while detail strengthens any claim, Worth was never known to have offered violence; indeed, his criminal *modus operandi* was never to have done so. It may be granted that he could have lived such a life at Landale without the disquieting Lyons episode, however, its presence as part of the story raises some question about the balance of the Elliott imposture. Certainly it must be acknowledged that Worth was quite capable of carrying off the life of an English gentleman, for he enjoyed a lifetime of imposture. There is a serious flaw in this theory, for it is has been established that he died in London with his two American children present. The present status of the Landale matter lies in the realm of the Scottish verdict of not proved, but the investigation of it should beckon as a delightful and appropriate challenge for some Sherlockian.

While Worth continued to plan nefarious activities for his associates, he continued, as he had put it, to "keep his hand in." Travelling to South Africa on his yacht, he set up an elaborate scheme to steal diamonds enroute from the mines to the boat. He developed a false persona as an ostrich feather buyer in a town which was on a river which had to be crossed, befriended the postmaster and stole the man's keys long enough to have them duplicated, then cut the ferry lose. Knowing the uncut diamonds would be placed in the postmaster's safe for the night, Worth entered at his leisure, removed them, and shipped them to England concealed in a shipment of ostrich feathers. His confederates formed a wholesale diamond establishment, selling the product to the diamond buyers who would have purchased them if they had not been purloined, thus avoiding the costly discount to the fences.

The second hands-on activity, and perhaps the most spectacular, but most certainly the least productive, was his personal theft of the celebrated Gainsborough portrait of the Duchess of Devonshire. No one has ever been able to explain his reason for breaking into the Agnew Gallery that night of May 27, 1876, with one of his minions, the seven foot tall, Jack "Junka" Phillips, who boosted him up to the second floor windows. The only explanation ever made was "because I want it." He left a small corner of the painting in the frame to establish the *bona fides* of the rest of the painting, rolled up the canvas and walked off with it. He kept the painting for the next twenty five years, usually concealed in the false bottom of a trunk, in England and later in America. It was this portrait which surely gave Doyle the idea of the Greuze painting of the young girl with the lamb behind Moriarty's desk.

Kitty, tired of being tied to a criminal life, left for New York with her two daughters, where she led a non-criminal life, ultimately marrying a Cuban-American millionaire, Juan Pedro Terry, who became the love of her life. They had a child and lived a life which was would later be called cafe-society, but which ended with the husband's early death. Kitty herself died at forty-two. Macintyre postulates that Worth kept the Gainsborough portrait because its "wilful, wileful gaze" reminded him of his lost Kitty.

It was generally understood at Scotland Yard and with the Pinkerton's that Worth had stolen the Duchess of Devonshire portrait, but they never could find it. One of Worth's favorite places was the Long Bar at the Criterion — note again the relationship with the Canon — where he was accosted by Phillips about the stolen picture.

Worth noted a Scotland Yard detective there in the background and concluded that Phillips had sold out. Worth ordered a bottle of champagne, struck Pillips over the head with it — not an inconsiderable feat due to their relative heights — and walked out.

Worth now made a capital mistake. Without proper planning, and on the spur of the moment, he robbed a mail wagon in Belgium. He was captured and sentenced to ten years. His old enemy, Max Shinburn, also in same prison, identified Worth to the authorities by his true name, and gave him a very bad time during Worth's imprisonment. Worth did not serve the full term, but by the time he was released, his health was broken (tuberculosis symptoms had appeared) and so was his spirit. He returned to England and learned that his assets were gone, and his henchman, Johnny Curtis, who was charged, according to Macintyre, to attend his wife, had seduced her and decamped with Worth's substantial assets, although other writers claim the funds were utilized by his henchmen to finance failed criminal activities. His wife, affected by all their reverses, was insane and in an asylum, although his wives tended to be, if substantial, shadowy, and probably the least confirmed areas of Worth's private life. Despite the depredations of his imprisonment, he was still able to mastermind two celebrated robberies: in 1897 a diamond merchant across the street from Worth's home in London, and the million franc robbery in the *Gare d' Nord* railway station in Paris in 1898. Although both were successful they were desperate enterprises as he badly needed immediate funds.

His son and daughter were still in the United States, his American wife dead, and he was not aging well, particularly with the increasing problems from tuberculosis. William Pinkerton arranged a meeting with Worth, and they found that they related well. Worth advised that he would have returned the Duchess painting years before if he had not been continually harrassed by one of the Scotland Yard inspectors, who was offensively following him. Finally,

Worth told Pinkerton "I think the Lady should return home, don't you?" Pinkerton quickly agreed. On March 18, 1901, the painting was returned. What was given in consideration thereof is not known, but since he returned to England, presumably it was a state of immunity.

On January 8, 1902, he died at age fifty-six, in his apartment which was either in Regents Park or in Camden, and either alone or with his two children with him. His children had been living in Brooklyn with his brother and sister-in-law since they were very young, and it is believed that he was obliged to send his last assets to his sister-in-law to obtain an agreement to send the children to him. Some reports placed his death in East London and in 1907, but I believe what I have first noted was the time and you can pick the place. Pinkerton, who had become quite close to Worth, furnished several hundred dollars to Worth's son, on the false but face-saving representation that he had recovered funds from some of Worth's debtors. He had come to care for Worth personally, which is perhaps the finest accolade which could be extended to an adversary across the deep gulf between them. Clearly, Worth was a finer adversary than was Moriarty.

There were some further ironies in the course of his children's lives. The younger daughter of Kitty was killed in a carriage-train accident in 1899, but the elder daughter and her son survived the accident. That grandson lived into our own day: he was Juan Trippe, who founded the famous but later ill-fated Pan American Airlines. Worth's son, Henry Raymond Jr. became a Pinkerton man.

NOTES

1. Rowan, Richard Wilmer, *The Pinkertons, A Detective Dynasty* (Little, Brown and Company: Boston), p. 272,273.
2. Page 281, Horan, James D., *The Pinkertons; the Detective Dynasty That Made History*, Crown Publishers, New York, 1969. However, at page 315 he refers to Worth's height at five feet five and a half. This was some years later, and it may have been that it was a consequence of ageing.

3. Like many impecunious and dishonest young men, he hired himself out as a substitute during the Civil War, receiving his bounty from the men for whom he was hired to be a substitute, enlisting, and then disappearing. Hiring a substitute was not an uncommon practice in the North, and apparently carried no social stigma. Young J.P. Morgan hired a substitute, thereby surviving both the war and any shame. It was a dirty practice, sanctioning wealth as it did, and in no later wars was it continued.
4. Felstead, S. Theodore, *Shades of Scotland Yard* (John Long Limited, London), p. 296.
5. Felstead, S. Theodore, *Shades of Scotland Yard* (John Long Limited, London).

The Maiden

THE MAIDEN plays a very special role in the Morality Play, the fairy tale and the melodrama, and is also the heroine in the latter two. She was always possessed of a delicate beauty, and represented a state of being sought by men who should know better than to regard her essential virginity as a challenge; for she was always appeared unattainable and, sorry, inviolate. Without drawing too fine a line, the very characteristic suggests the name: inviolate transformed into Violet.

There are fewer candidates for the Ur-Violet than for her sister, the heroine; indeed I know of no one who has felt that such speculation was worthwhile. Yet to take this approach misses some very instructive byways, for Violets appear and reappear throughout the long life of the Canon. We are offered Violets de Merville, Hunter, Smith and Westbury.

There was surely something appealing to Doyle in the name Violet. That was apparent not only from the number invested by him with that name but also from the deportment of the Canonical ladies themselves. Admittedly, Violet Westbury was a cipher, not even being permitted a direct quotation, but all of the others were women of decisiveness, beauty, character, courage, and a certain peremptoriness. Miss Hunter, who did not know Holmes, sent him a letter advising that she would be calling on him at half-past ten tomorrow. She did not request an appointment, she ordered it. Now, it is true that she did qualify the meeting with the caveat, if she did not inconvenience him, but that was only a polite female word formula.

Later she was even more peremptory in directing Holmes to come to Winchester; indeed, John Watson characterized it as a "summons." Holmes called her "a very brave and sensible girl," but admittedly that was after she had advised him that she had lain "awake half the night at the thought of seeing you."

Watson described Violet Smith as being a "young and beautiful woman, tall, graceful and queenly," She was a cyclist, in fact, the solitary cyclist, and at a time when women cyclists were regarded as the bra burners of a later day.

Violet de Merville was limned by Colonel Damery as "young, rich, beautiful, accomplished, wonder-woman in every way." Her icy, controlled presence in the face of the warning warmth of Holmes' strong strictures against Baron Gruner well illustrated her mettle.

Who was the original of the fictive Violets? Or, more properly, was there an original? The answer is yes to both questions.

Many a pleasant evening was spent with Michael Harrison over companionable brandies discussing the Ur-Violet. He was satisfied that he knew her identity and I'm convinced that he was right; indeed, their lives had overlapped as she had not died until 1937. And in that peculiar circular circuity of matters Holmesian, which virtually mandates that certain matters, like murder, will out, one of her castles was Haddon Hall, that celebrated Elizabethan pile in Derbyshire which is one of the two sites suggested as the rural seat of the Duke of Holdernesse.

Michael's choice was the wife of the eighth Duke of Rutland, a woman well known socially and artistically in late Victorian, Edwardian and Georgian England; so well known that it would have been difficult to have not to have heard of her and her activities. Her name? Violet, of course, Violet Manners.

She was born Violet Lindsay, to a rich family related to the aristocracy but neither as aristocratic nor as wealthy as their friends. She lived a country-house kind of life on the family estate near Wantage, some sixty miles westerly of

London. Wantage remains today a small Berkshire town of under ten thousand people, beautifully situated in the Vale of the White Horse. The birthplace of Alfred the Great, it was a charming area in which to be born, for both Alfred and Violet.

Violet was a beautiful child who became a beautiful young woman, graceful and accomplished. She was fortunate in living at a time when her face fulfilled what was regarded as the classic lines and coloring, and she has been described as possessing a Pre-Raphaelite beauty.

Taught the womanly accomplishments of her class, which were arts of sketching, music and conversation, she had an attractive singing voice and accompanied herself on the piano, but it was in drawing and sculpture which she excelled, and it was said that had she not been a member of the upper classes, her artistry would have received more serious recognition, although the fact that her work in both mediums was acquired by museums in England and France evidences a not insignificant artistic acceptance.

Not a well-read woman, she was intelligent rather than intellectual, but did travel in intellectual circles, becoming a member of the famous group known at the "Souls." It was a celebrated aggregation of very bright young London aristocrats who were later characterized by her daughter, Diana Cooper, as "a group of intelligent, cultured men and women, who knew how to live and love and serve and savor the best..."[1] Like most us, Lady Diana was a prisoner of her time and place and class, and so likened the group to the Cafe Society to which she belonged — she and her husband were friends of Edward VIII and were passengers on his Mediterranean yachting party with Mrs. Simpson — but the Souls were far more inquiring and intellectual and talented than Edward VIII and his generally vapid Dorchester and Belvedere crowd. The Souls included many of the later movers and shakers of Britain.

Violet married well, a handsome young man named Henry Manners, who was of the family who were the Dukes of Rutland; landed and wealthy, and who later became the eighth Duke. Henry was not particularly ambitious, preferring a more social and non-celebrated life, but he did become the Principal Private Secretary to Lord Salisbury when the latter was Prime Minister.

The aristocrats have always possessed their own code of sexual behavior, which was one of modified license, that is, modified only by avoiding public displays. There was a prevalent adage that one could do what one liked in a carriage, so long as one did not scare the horses. Decorum was vital, but was an acceptable social cover for infidelity. Appearance was the test, not allegiance, and as one writer recently observed as to Prince Philip, he owed his wife loyalty and not fidelity. Quite often among the aristocrats, however, there was neither. The marriage of the Manners' was no exception, both strayed but both kept their infidelities within the close confines and knowledge of their class. There was no boasting but there were no admissions either, and it was generally recognized, even by the product of that long affair, that Diana Cooper was the daughter of Henry Cust, also one of the Souls, and the acknowledged regency rakehell of the time. Lady Diana noted in her autobiography that she drew comfort from reading *Tom Jones*.

VIOLET MANNERS
DUCHESS OF RUTLAND

It is not known whether Conan Doyle knew of Violet's infidelities, or if knowing, cared the less for her. He himself loved a woman other than his first wife, but that relationship was known by his and her intimates, including his mother, and no one ever claimed that it was sexual. Doyle remained with his consumptive wife until her death, and he was regarded by all as a man of immense integrity in all things. Just as he could look beyond what he regarded as the sickness of homosexuality in friends such as Sir Roger

Casement and Oscar Wilde, and support them both publicly and privately, he may well have felt the same about Violet Manners' sexual promiscuity. But the point is not what he knew or didn't know, but that he had come to regard her as representing the very flower of all things beautifully and elegantly feminine.

The great tragedy of Violet's life was the death of her nine year old son, Haddon — named after Haddon Hall, I'm sure — she acknowledged to her daughter in her eighties that she still felt his loss as keenly but did not think about it as often. His mother sought to work through her immediate grief by doing a beautiful sculpture of her dead son, recumbent, the original cast of which is in the Tate gallery with the marble final production in the chapel at Haddon Hall. It is a magnificent piece of work, and in my untutored view is as fine as the famous statues of David or Pauline Bonaparte or the Pieta.

Violet Manners died in her eighties in 1937, her husband having predeceased her in 1925.

Henry Manners first became duke-apparent as Lord Granby and then the Duke of Rutland, and with his accession to the dukedom, he and his family lived at Belvoir Castle, pronounced British-like as Beaver, one of the stately homes of the kingdom. While Belvoir was the seat, they, of course spent was called "the season' in their London home, and the eighth Duchess of Rutland was much in the newspapers because of her beauty and her position. It was not surprising that Doyle was enamored of her, albeit distantly.

She was regarded by all as the most elegant duchess of them all, lithe, beautiful, gifted, artistic and charming. She was the dream of many Englishmen of her day, and like the stuff of most dreams, unattainability tended to add its own particular enchantment. Doyle was no different.

* * *

There is another candidate, although one marginally not as serious. She is another Violet, one whose full name suggests strong entitlements, Miss Violet Hunt.

I first learned of her from Paul Brundage, a fellow Irregular, who had read a book in which I wrote, with Violet Hunt as the pseudonymous author.[2] He sent me a book about Violet Hunt, entitled *Violet*, by Barbara Belford,[3] and bearing the heavy subtitle of "the story of the irrepressible Violet Hunt and her circle of lovers and friends — Ford Madox Ford, H.G.Wells, Somerset Maugham, Ezra Pound, Rebecca West, John Ruskin, Wyndham Lewis, Radclyffe Hall, Joseph Conrad, John Galsworthy, Thomas hardy, Arnold Bennett and Henry James."

VIOLET HUNT

She was born in 1862 in Durham, to Alfred and Margaret Hunt, he a painter and she a novelist. Moving the family to London in 1866, their home of Tor Villa was a popular one with the likes of John Ruskin and Oscar Wilde. Violet was an intellectual and a sybarite who cloaked in proper Victorian rectitude her blazing private life. Although she was willing to share her sexual favors, it was only for interesting men to whom she devoted her love. Her loyalty was fierce and if she repeatedly violated the Victorian taboos it was generally in private and with men for whom she loved, and whom she wished to marry, but who were, unfortunately, generally already married Equally unfortunately, when their wives died or were divorced, they always married other women. She could have easily become a man-hater or a follower of her friend, the noted and notable lesbian, Radclyffe Hall, but she became neither, and soon there was another male lover, and married, of course.

Almost a beautiful woman, with a face often characterized as being Pre-Raphaelite, it was her manner and intelligence which was most compelling. In love with Oscar Wilde as a young girl, he termed her "the sweetest violet in England." She became, at her instance, the lover of

George Broughton when she was twenty-two and he, fifty-one and married. He was a successful painter and a member of the Royal Academy. The relationship continued for some years, and thereafter she became the lover of Oswald John Frederick Crawfurd, the editor of a magazine and publishing company, and also married. He urged her to write and was influential in publishing her first book in 1894, *The Maiden's Progress*. Other books followed, *A Hard Woman, Way of Marriage, Unkist, Unkind, The Human Interest, Affairs of the Heart, Sooner or Later*, and then in 1908 *White Rose of Weary Leaf*, which was regarded as the work which made her artistic reputation.

Crawfurd was not faithful either to his mistress or his wife, and Violet, disheartened, ended the relationship which she had hoped would lead to marriage. In *Sooner or Later*, she wrote about their affair, even using their actual dialogue, and it constituted a catharsis for her.

She had maintained a diary since she was fourteen and its frankness was either refreshing or repulsive, depending upon your particular prejudice. One entry observed: "My idea of a lover is a man whose first care is his mistress — his greatest happiness her company — his greatest obligation her happiness."

Her books were personal and dealt with the manifold problems of women. *Unkist* was described as "a gothic tale about weak men and strong women," and *The Human Interest* was stated to be an English reflection of Flaubert's *Bovary*.[4]

She became the lover of Somerset Maugham in 1905, and when he was gone Arnold Bennett squired her around. *White Rose* was dedicated to Maugham and in his *Moon and Sixpence* she was the character of Rose Waterford, a beautiful novelist who had both charm and a viciousness. She and Maugham remained close friends after their passion ended.

Henry James was also her friend, but it was a non-sexual relationship. H.G. Wells was both friend and lover, lover at first and thereafter friend. Young Ezra Pound was also a friend. Not surprisingly, she was a suffragette, but not a violent one.

She wrote for the *Black and White* magazine, which often carried her picture because she was a public figure. She also wrote for *Sphere* and the *Tatler*, as well as other periodicals. Douglas Goldring wrote that she was "one of the outstanding women writers of the period, and, within the limitations of her particular world, she 'knew everyone' and 'went everywhere'...." She was, "one of the most exciting figures in the Edwardian capital. Fashionable, brilliant, daring."[5]

In 1907 she met Ford Maddox Hueffer (much later changed to Ford Maddox Ford) at a dinner party given by John Galsworthy, and soon they became lovers, she at age 46 and he at age 35. She wrote in her diary "I was full, not of love, but of loving — kindness and obsessed by the permanent illusion of all women that they can save."[6] Hueffer, like all her lovers, was married, and this affair become public knowledge. There was libel litigation in 1913, instituted by Hueffer's wife over whether he had divorced her and whether he and Violet were married. They lost many friends, who were embarrassed by the flaunting of societal standards. Although unmarried, they lived as husband and wife for some years, but ultimately separated amid continuing and great bitterness. Hueffer continued the pattern of rejection, taking a different woman as his lover.

Violet was a character in many of Hueffer's books and her book, *Their Lives*, continued her autobiographical novels. There were more books through the years, and in the 1920's she wrote two books of a different *genre*, these departures being *Tales of the Uneasy* and *More Tales of the Uneasy*. Other works were also regularly published, including an autobiography and in 1932 her final book, entitled *The Wife of Rossetti*. In that circle of Sherlockian connections, she started, but did not finish, a biography of Charles Augustus Howell.

Evelyn Waugh perceptively characterized her novels as sad, "Some of bitterness, some of resignation, always, though, of courage, always of unfulfillment, with, at the close, now and again a note of lonely triumph."[7] She died in 1937, the same year as the other Violet, the Duchess of Rutland. And, shades of Doyle, she wrote a book in 1910 entitled — are you ready for this — *The Wife of Altamont*.

It is not known if she had ever met Doyle, but they were both well-known writers in the confines of a rather small country, and an even smaller class. Was Doyle influenced sufficiently to borrow part of her name in any of his stories? I think not, but it must remain a mystery, subject to the opening of Doyle's papers after an unconscionable period of sixty-five years, however we can be sure that if the Violet was borrowed, the Hunt(er) was not, for Miss Violet Hunter first appeared in the *Copper Beeches* in June of 1892, with the writing occurring at some unknown date before that, and Miss Hunt was neither generally nor recognizably known either as a person or a writer before 1894. It is possible that Doyle may have met her before then, but the possibilities are completely speculative without recourse to the elusive Doyle papers.

Which was the Ur-Violet? Probably the Duchess of Rutland, because of the greater likelihood of Doyle's knowledge and the demands of the dates. But either was certainly a woman well worth admiration from afar, and probably also up close.

So it was that one of two celebrated Pre-Raphaelite ladies, who shared more attributes than society would require either to admit, so stirred a young writer at the age of thirty three that the same feeling remained for an old writer of sixty five.

NOTES

1. Cooper, Lady Diana, *The Rainbow Comes and Goes*, Rupert Hart-Davis, London, 1958.
2. *Skewed Sherlock*, Hunter, Violet, and Hammer, David, Gasogene Press, Dubuque, 1992.
3. Published by Simon and Schuster, New York, 1990.

4. Page 108, Belford, Barbara, *Violet*, Simon and Schuster, New York, 1990.
5. Page 135, Belford. Barbara, *Violet*, Simon and Schuster, New York 1990.
6. *Ibid*, page 150.
7. *Ibid*, page 255.

The Premier

THE PREMIER was the surrogate of the king in life as well as in melodrama and Miracle Plays. Today he is not only the surrogate but the possessor of all the power of the king, to whom only the right to advise and warn remain.

In the United Kingdom, of which Holmes was a subject, the first minister is variously termed the prime minister or the premier. The latter is a French designation, long accepted in England as one of the portmanteau terms from France which arrived in England after 1066 and which, like many other terms, became acceptably English.

We know that four cases brought Holmes in contact with the then prime ministers, and during the reigns of three sovereigns, Queen Victoria, King Edward and King George. The cases were *The Adventure of the Second Stain*, *The Adventure of the Bruce-Partington Plans*, *The Adventure of the Mazarin Stone*, and *His Last Bow*.

When did these cases occur? The chronologists offer a long time spread for *Stain*, from 1886 through 1894, November 1895 for *Bruce*, the summer of 1903 or 1904 for *Mazarin*, and August 1914 for *Last Bow*.

The second inquiry should be into the ministerial terms bridging the times of the cases.

Prime Ministerial Date Table

DATES	PRIME MINISTER
February-July 1886	William Ewart Gladstone
August 1886-July 1892	3rd Marquess of Salisbury
July 1892-March 1894	William Ewart Gladstone

March 1894–June 1895	5th Earl of Rosebery
June 1895–July 1902	3rd Marquess of Salisbury
July 1902–December 1905	A.J. Balfour
December 1905–February 1908	Sir Henry Campbell-Bannerman
February 1908–December 1916	H.H. Asquith

Holmes' first recorded meeting with a prime minister occurred at the beginning of the *Adventure of the Second Stain*.

"It was then, in a year, and even a decade, that shall be nameless, that upon one Tuesday morning in autumn we found two visitors of European fame within the walls of our humble room in Baker Street. The one, austere, high-nosed, eagle-eyed, and dominant was none other than the illustrious Lord Bellinger, twice premier of Britain."

The time spread, from 1886 to 1894, encompasses the prime ministerships of Salisbury, once, and Gladstone, twice. Robert Arthur Talbot Gascoyne-Cecil, third Marquess of Salisbury, thrice prime minister of Britain, was born in 1830 and died in 1903. An aristocrat, being a member of the famous Cecil family (pronounced sisal, like the hemp), which had produced leaders for their country for many generations. Educated at Eton and Oxford, being intended for an academic career, bad health required a long sea journey, and when he returned to England from around the world he was elected to Parliament, which became his professional life. A strict conservative, he was appointed Secretary of State for India, but a year later, in 1867, he resigned over the Second Reform Bill which was pushed by Benjamin Disraeli, whom he distrusted. The next year, on the death of his father, he became the third marquess of Salisbury, and therefore succeeded to the House of Lords. When Disraeli became prime minister in 1874 he returned to the India post, and thereafter, until the end of his life, he was involved in foreign affairs, a subject in which he had both an interest and a speciality. Indeed, during his first two terms as prime minister, which covered the years involved in the *Second Stain* investigation, he also acted as foreign

MARQUESS OF SALISBURY

minister,[1] thus he would not have needed the services of the Right Honourable Trelawney Hope, the foreign secretary who appeared at Baker Street with the premier. This fact would alone militate against the selection of Salisbury as the original of prime minister Bellinger who visited Baker Street and retained Holmes' services.

There is a second reason, and that is the physical description of Bellinger. Salisbury was moon-faced, not at all angular, and his most noticeable facial feature was a full and dark beard. No, he was not Lord Bellinger; his closest connection was that both were aristocrats.

In a way I have not played fair with you, for it was clear from the start that Doyle intended that Bellinger was to be William Ewart Gladstone, and the physical description alone would have quickly betrayed his identity to any late Victorian Englishman. Austere, high-nosed and eagle-eyed, are terms which described Gladstone definitively. Of middle height, described as handsome when young, he remained the spare-bodied person he was as a young man, but his face became craggy as he aged, so that he could pass for what we regard as a Roman senator, complete with the high nose properly characterized as Roman. But it was his fierce dark eyes which dominated both his face and his fellows. Viscount John Morley, a Liberal politician who penned his official biography, referred to "his falcon's eye with its strange imperious flash." Doyle's selection of the term "eagle-eyed" was deliberate, and that alone would be sufficient to identify the original of Bellinger to any percipient reader, and we all are quick to recognize that all of his readers were easily and exceptionally percipient.

Gladstone, born in 1809 in Liverpool, was of Scottish

descent and the name was the non-gladsome one of Gladstones, which was not changed until he was in Parliament. His father was a self-made wealthy shipper, and Gladstone was thus a child of what the Germans call burgertum. Rebuffed twice with offers of marriage, he was a most fortunate man, because his third offer was to Miss Catherine Glynne of Hawarden, the daughter of a land-owning baronet, which was accepted.

WILLIAM GLADSTONE

Both socially and politically it was an important step above his merchant background, but more importantly, she was an intelligent, charming and supportive young woman, who devoted herself to his interests. Even in old age she was a strikingly handsome woman. They had a good marriage and eight children.

Gladstone was strongly Anglican and had intended to become a clergyman but his father influenced him to enter politics, although the son approached that work as a religious enterprise. He was either high-minded or bloody-minded, depending upon the political persuasion of the critic, but history records him as being a man of principle who also sought to act with principle. There were no intellectual shortcuts for Gladstone. Beginning as a Tory, his thought processes gradually moved him into the Liberal party, and it was as a Liberal that he was four times the sovereign's prime minister, the first time at age 59 and the last at age 82. He was an "old, wild and incomprehensible man" according to his Queen, who did not like him. She preferred the unctuous Disraeli or the aristocrats to Gladstone, complaining that he addressed her "as if I was a public meeting."

He was a commanding speaker who used persuasion to sell people on principle, carrying them on his orotund waves of oratory, or, as his adversary Disraeli phrased it, "inebriated by the exuberance of his own verbosity." His speeches in the House as well as on the hustings were long, usually one to two hours, but they did contain eloquence as well as tedium.[2] In the 1866 electoral reform debate he ended his oration: "*Excoriare aliquis nostris ex ossibus ultor.* You cannot fight against the future. Time is on our side. The great social forces which move onwards in their might and majesty...are against you."[3]

A graduate of Eton and Oxford, he was an educated man, writing one book in three volumes on Plato, stressing his Pre-Christian teachings, and another even duller book on the Church Of England.

Religion played a large role in his life, from his tediousness of principle to self-flagellation when he was younger, to his late evening talks with prostitutes, seeking to assist them to change their profession. That he was not misunderstood in this frequent venture easily attests to the recognition of his rock-ribbed integrity. He was a brilliant Chancellor of the Exchequer, perhaps the most complicated of ministries, and was no less skillful as Prime Minister.

The Irish issue came to dominate his ministries and his private life alike; a cause which he convinced his party to espouse reluctantly, and which ultimately split it. He also sought to assist in the unification of Italy and the freedom of the Bulgarians. He easily spoke in terms of "mission." His wife, in the middle of their lives together once told him: "Oh William, dear, if you weren't such a great man you would be a terrible bore."

Retiring in 1890 from Commons, where he had served for sixty-two years, he returned to his wife's estate of Hawarden in Flintshire, beloved by him. He had, years before, saved Hawarden from financial ruin by his wife's family and through the years had increased its size substantially. He died there in 1898.

Lord Wilson, a 20th century successor to the prime ministership,[4] wrote in his book about prime ministers, "Gladstone was a massive character, yet one of the most psychologically complicated personalities in the whole history of Britain's fifty Prime Ministers." Wilson also noted that "he had a contempt for political manoeverings. For him politics...was the realization of theological imperatives which were revealed to him..."[5]

Perhaps the most telling fact about Gladstone was that he was the favorite of the people rather than the aristocracy, and he became so well known as the Grand Old Man that it was unnecessary to write it out, as the initials GOM were sufficient to identify him. For reasons unknown to this day, but probably due to his religious feeling and his essential modesty, he repeatedly refused a knighthood or other preferment, living and dying simply as William Gladstone, or if you prefer, the GOM.

* * *

It was the third week of November in the year 1895 when a puzzled Watson met Holmes' brother, Mycroft, who was characterized by Holmes as "the most indispensable man in the country." He may have been right, for as the *Adventure of the Bruce-Partington Plans* developed Watson came to respect Mycroft's thoroughness. In the course of the Mycroftian discourse, Mycroft observed that "I have never seen the Prime Minister so upset."

That Prime Minister does not otherwise obtrude into the story, and it is not important for us, because he was the Marquess of Salisbury, whom we met a bit earlier. Had it been earlier in the year the Prime Minister would have been Archibald Philip Primrose, the fifth Earl of Rosebery, who was nominated by the Queen herself, a most unusual action, and who was never in the House of Commons but always in the House of Lords. He disliked politics and served as the first minister for only a few months. He had married a Rothschild, thus wiving wealthily, and happily. He was an eloquent public speaker, but after the early death of his wife he had little interest in life, other than his three Derby wins at Epsom, and he was forced by his friends and family into politics. He was not without charm, but it could turn into acid, as when his wife's visiting family was not ready to end the day and go to bed, he peremptorily quoted the Old Testament, "To your tents, O Israel."

* * *

In the summer of 1904 or 1905, depending upon which chronologer you accept, that very odd case, *The Adventure of the Mazarin Stone*, occurred. It has never received the imprimatur of the serious adepts, and for good reason.

There is a reference by young Billy the page to the Prime Minister and the Home Secretary sitting on Holmes' sofa in his quarters at Baker Street. The Prime Minister, regardless of whether you opt for 1904 or 1905, would have been Arthur James Balfour.

He was the nephew of the Marquess of Salisbury, and had been in effect the Prime Minister for the latter portion of his uncle's premiership.

EARL OF BALFOUR

Balfour, subsequently named the Earl of Balfour, was born in 1848, and attended both Eton and Cambridge. He was an aristocrat with a brilliant mind, and the author of *Defence of Philosophic Doubt* and *The Foundations of Belief*, both books being analyses of the assumptions upon which science is based. The Marquess of Salisbury prevailed upon him to enter Commons as a Tory, and afforded him increasing responsibilities.

The tragedy of his life was the death of his intended fiance a month after their engagement; he never married. Regarded by most as "a languid exquisite, rather than a man of action, an amusing and witty social figure no doubt, but one of the last people for whom political success could have been predicted. He moved in a circle of rich, clever and delightful men and women —'The Souls' — a brilliant society of which he was a central figure."[6]

In July 1902 he became premier *de jure* as well as *de facto*, resigning at the end of 1905. He commenced many new initiatives aimed at preparing the country for the threat of Wilhelmine Germany, one of which was the Anglo-French Convention of 1904, constituting a profound departure from England's historic adverse relationship with France. He performed many services for his country after his premiership, including becoming foreign secretary in 1916 under David Lloyd George, who had been one of his most severe critics. After the war he became Lord President of the Council and died in 1930.

* * *

The last prime ministerial connection with Mr. Holmes was chronicled by him in *His Last Bow*. In 1912 the Premier and the Foreign Secretary came to his South Down cottage with a proposal to serve King and country. "The Foreign Minister alone I could have withstood, but when the Premier also deigned to visit my humble roof —! The fact is, Watson, that this gentleman upon the sofa was a bit too good for our people. He was in a class by himself."[7]

HERBERT HENRY ASQUITH

This observation was an author's tell. Doyle, like the premier, Herbert Henry Asquith, was a Liberal, and Doyle had run unsuccessfully as a Liberal on two occasions. Asquith was Prime Minister from 1908 until 1916, and was responsible for England's New Deal program before the Great War. It was the first time taxation was used for social rather than revenue purposes, and a substantive social welfare program instituted in a shrewdly designed Parliamentary ploy.

Asquith was born in Lancashire in 1852. His father was a small businessman and a Congregationalist who died when the son was eight, and the son's education was by scholarship. He was graduated from Balliol College at Oxford with the highest honors. Thereafter he was called to the Bar and became a successful barrister, combining that profession with being a member of the House of Commons, as did so many other bright young advocates. He became Chancellor of the Exchequer in a Liberal administration in 1905, remaining there for three years, when he became Premier.

Asquith was alert to the German threat and did much to prepare England for the coming war, which was a subtle reason to introduce him into the Canon in the way it was done and in the precise connection but without naming him.

In 1916 Asquith was toppled by a party coup involving his second in command, David Lloyd George, who succeeded him as Premier. Asquith was made a Knight of the Garter and a peer in 1925, taking the title of 1st Lord of Oxford and Asquith. Whether one approves of his social program or not, he is to be admired for the shrewd manner in which he accomplished it, and no one disapproved of his efforts to prepare England for the war which he recognized as coming. It is most natural that someone like Doyle, another poor boy who conquered the ramparts, would find common cause with Asquith. The Have-nots had defeated the Haves and all for the good of the Neverhads. It is no wonder that Doyle choose to have Holmes observe that the Premier was in a class by himself.

NOTES

1. Salisbury, being more interested in foreign matters than domestic, accomplished little domestically, which was quite satisfactory to him as a conservative. He did accomplish much in the field of external affairs. He was an imperialist, extending British colonies in Africa.

2. The eloquence is illustrated in a speech with dangerous implications in 1862, when, in reference to the Confederate Sates of

America, he proclaimed "There is no doubt that Jefferson Davis and other leaders of the South have made an army; they are making, it appears, a navy; and they have made what is more difficult than either, they have made a nation."

3. Jenkins, Roy, *Gladstone* (Random House: New York, 1997), p. 376.
4. Wilson, Harold, *A Prime Minister on Prime Ministers* (Summit Books: New York, 1977).
5. *Ibid*, page 127.
6. *Encyclopedia Britannica*, v, 3, Chicago, 1966.
7. Doyle, A. Conan, *The Complete Sherlock Holmes* (Barnes & Noble: New York, 1992), Page 978.

The Prince

NO RESPECTABLE FAIRY TALE, which shares its lineage as a progeny of the Miracle Plays, the precursor of melodrama, can successfully function without a prince. Indeed, we now also possess a frog prince.

There was no question who the prince was in the Sherlock Holmes stories. He was not the young prince but a middle-aged one, Albert Edward, the Prince of Wales, born in 1841, the eldest son of Albert, the Prince Consort, and the Queen, Victoria.

Doyle, self-circumscribed by the bounds of the code of a gentleman, as well as by his duty to the monarchy, limited Albert Edward to a brief allusion in *The Adventure of the Illustrious Client*. He was, in fact, that illustrious client. That client bore, as Sir James Damery explained, an "honoured name." Although he declined to identify the client further, Watson saw, at the conclusion of the case, the armorial bearings on the carriage carrying Sir James, and before he could identify the client, Holmes interjected "It is a loyal friend and a chivalrous gentleman.... Let that now and forever be enough for us." And so it was. I suspect the armorial bearings observed by Watson were the well-known and easily-identified ones of the Prince of Wales, containing the celebrated three feathers.

There is, not unexpectedly, a time problem, for the date given was September 3, 1902, which month and year is agreed to by all of the chronologists. It was the year previous when the Prince of Wales became the King-Emperor. If the date for the adventure is correct, then I should not be permitted, in the interests of accuracy, to regard the King as the Prince. There are two justifications for this: first, many of the Holmes cases occurred when he was Prince of Wales; and second, I suspect that the date used by Watson was obfuscatory. If it was in fact 1902 then George would have been the Prince of Wales and he was not temperamentally suited to have done what Sir James Damery's principal did.

EDWARD VII
PRINCE OF WALES

Physically, he was not impressive; below today's medium height, increasingly rotund, blue-eyed, with his receding Hanoverian chin concealed behind a beard.

The Prince of Wales was more German than English, his father being German and his mother's mother was German. The Hanoverians themselves, his ancestors, were also German, and George I spoke no English. The Prince of Wales himself spoke English with a German accent, which is not surprising as German was the family language of his parents and their home. Yet, despite all this Germanicism, he became an essentially English king.

His father, the Prince Consort, visited him at Cambridge University because of certain of his difficulties there, and returning to Windsor Castle, the Prince Consort died there soon after of typhoid fever. The Queen unreasonably blamed the son for the father's death, when she should have blamed the antiquated drains at Windsor. Worse, she held her son in some contempt, for not unreasonable considerations, giving obvious preference to other children, particularly to his brother Leopold. Despite the requests of several premiers, she refused to give him any information regarding government and certainly no responsibility.

The Ottoman practice of locking a royal opponent in the harem for several years resulted, not unexpectedly, in babbling idiots, such as the last Turkish sultan, who preferred to chew watermelon seeds. The practice of denying the Prince of Wales any governmental responsibilities whatsoever had an effect similar to the seraglio commitments in Turkey. If the prince did not chew watermelon seeds like his Turkish counterpart, he did embrace women, gambling, hunting and practical jokes, none of which constitutes serious preparation for a productive life; this was his life until he was sixty years of age.

He married Princess Alexandra of Denmark, beautiful but bland, who became a possessive mother, even requiring her adult children to address her as "Motherdear." Like many women, she transferred her affection from her husband to her children.

She was a nineteenth century royal, however, accepting as part of the essential business of royalty marriage without love as a constitutient of the bargain; indeed, it only complicated an otherwise professional relationship. Unfortunately, some twentieth century royals permitted themselves to be too naive to accept this ancient doctrine.

The female royal was obliged to remain, in the term of the time, pure, for there could be adulteration in the succession, or alternatively, careful. Once, however, the succession was abundantly assured there was nothing to prohibit the royal male from spreading his royal seed without hazard to the monarchy, and the royal female from finding courtiers who would attend to her, provided it was done discreetly and without either publication or issue. The inhibitions attending to the royal female did not extend to the royal male; indeed, the ladies attending to him were well known and their progress was watched with interest, not unlike our American sports figures.

In England, the royal bastards were identified by the prefix Fitz, and not only was there no social stigma but rather there was a social cachet.[1] It has only been in our own day when, to sell newspapers and newsbites, the personal life of a sovereign and the other royals has come to be regarded as public news.

The role of the royal consort was clearly defined, and as it was known, so was it easier to fulfill. She, first of all, saw nothing, realized nothing and what wasn't seen or heard could be easily ignored as nonexistent. Alexandra fulfilled her royal role superbly, even assisting her husband's lovers or former lovers by extending to them the grace of her station. After Lillie Langtry committed an unpardonable *lese majestie* by putting ice down the neck of the Prince of Wales at a ball, she was immediately cut by what was termed society, however, the Princess of Wales called upon her at her home, in a kind and generous gesture. Some years later, when her husband, the King, was dying, she brought Mrs. Alice Keppel, his most longstanding mistress, to his bedside, and then withdrew. Now that was the royal touch. More years later, during the short reign of their grandson, Edward VIII, the same Mrs. Keppel was heard to observe about Mrs. Wallis Simpson, that "we did things better in my day." In our own day, the descendent of Mrs. Keppel, Camilla Parker-Bowles, and the descendant of Edward VII, the current Prince of Wales, have established an arcanely atavistic activity, having the same relationship enjoyed by their progenitors, thus observing the Eliadean myth of the eternal return. Unfortunately for the current prince, the news media intruders have successfully changed the rules on the royals, thus hazarding his succession and perhaps the monarchy itself, and all because the people have bought too deeply into the fairytale myths of Prince Charming and of living happily ever after. So it seems that an institution may be hazarded from a too great belief in its now perceived ethos. Thus do ideas still control institutions.

Albert Edward hated the Albert part of his name, and refused his mother's insistence that he reign in that double name. As both Wales and King he was what the French characterize as a *bon vivant*, a *flaneur* and a *boulevardier*. Of course, the Parisians understood him and his ways. A man of taste, he was a *gourmet* and then a *gourmand*, still not an uncommon progression, as his increasing girth testified, despite heroic measures by his tailor. He was called Tum-Tum, generally to his back and when it was occasionally otherwise, he was not amused, and the offender was cut from the royal presence.

Apparel was important to him, as it is with those who deal in decorum, and uniforms and decorations had to be appropriate. Precedence was also quite naturally important to the royals, as they went first. Once at Windsor, when he was still Prince of Wales and Kaiser Wilhelm of Germany was still Crown Prince, the latter vehemently objected to him when the King of Tonga, a man of high color, was seen to appear to enter the dining room immediately after Queen Victoria. Wilhelm felt he should enter before a black king ruling a small island, and Wales advised him that "either the fellow was a blackamoor or a king, and as no blackamoor would be invited to the palace he had to be a king, and a king preceded both of them."

The list of his mistresses is not as long as one would suppose; not because he was abstinent but simply because in the fashion of the day his personal life was protected by palace and press alike. Although there were many women in his personal life — he preferred to talk to women than to men, and to be with them — which in the England of his day was quite a compliment to them and to him. As to his paramours, they were divided into those who appeared at court and those who did not, and while there were more in the latter group they were not as well known, save for the famous *cocottes* like Cora Pearl and La Belle Otero, and the consummate actress, Sarah Bernhardt, but they didn't not stay the course as long. The court beauties were well known, not only personally but in their relationships with the Prince, including Lillie Langtry, Daisy, the Duchess of Warwick, Mrs. Greville, the Duchess of Marlborough, Mrs. George Keppel, Lady Londonderry, Mrs. Arthur Sassoon, Mrs. Willie James, Lady Troubridge, Lady Mordaunt, Mrs. Corwallis-West, and Lady Lonsdale.

Except for Lillie Langtry, the court beauties were all related to the higher aristocracy, usually being married to younger sons of non-royal dukes, but all were intelligent, beautiful and accomplished. All were married and their husbands were not troublesome, for the Prince was favored by the feudal concept of duty to royalty, which was a attenuated approach to the earlier feudal right, rendered in English as the right of the first night, whereby the feudal leader was permitted to enjoy the favors of a lower-born bride the first night of her marriage. Although not a democratic concept, it was apparently democratic in operation. While this particular feudal right was long gone in the England of Prince Albert Edward, the concept survived in the matter of a husband accepting the interest and dalliance of the Crown in his wife, which required a discrete ignorance. It is not something which Americans can appreciate, but this acceptance as a subject to the crown is not unrelated to the American rite of ravishment by the Internal Revenue — I refuse to term it a service.

In the short reign of Edward VII, his first act was to drop forever the name Albert, undoubtedly largely because of his mother's expressed wish that he rule as Albert I. His reign was generally unproductive, except for one event which was pivotal, and that was the abandonment of England's historic policy of splendid isolation and its pact with its ancient enemy, France. The King was not only involved in this national realignment, but more than that, was influential therein. Now it was true that uncle and nephew, Edward and Wilhelm, regarded each other with a certain reciprocal hostility, and that was certainly significant, but there was more than that for Edward was attracted to France. For years he had loved Paris and enjoyed its free and easy ways. Paris, for its part, enthusiastically responded to he whom they called the Prince de Galles. So it was that, as so often in history, a particular corner is turned because of an attitude.

Edward, Prince and King, involved himself in the problems of his friends, sometimes disastrously, thus the de Merville matter would have been quite consistent with his demonstrable conduct. Doyle knew his sovereign's frailties, his fancies and his feelings, and his portrayal was truthful, but guarded. Doyle, the gentleman, and Doyle the subject, were both mindful of their duty to the Crown, and he would never have put the royal family at hazard, much less at a questionable disadvantage. Thus it was that in the cavalcade of the Canon, there is included a king, albeit decorously.

NOTES

1. There is another Sherlockian connection here. One of the most eloquent writers was Michael Hardwick, who was a descendant of the father of Queen Victoria, but conceived, and it was delicately phrased in those days, on the wrong side of the sheets.

The Duke

THOSE FAIRY TALES with princes usually also provide dukes, and such nobles, while explicably absent from American melodrama, are not absent from the Everyman Morality Plays.

There are not many dukes in the Canon, so the Duke of Holdernesse stands forth as an easy exemplar. Young Clay claimed a royal duke in his lineage, but that was a peripheral observation unburdened by proof.

The Duke of Holdernesse was introduced to Mr. Holmes and Dr. Watson by the distraught headmaster at the Priory School in Hallamshire, usually rendered as Derbyshire, which county has been colloquially referred to as the Dukeries because of the number of dukes resident there. We are told that His Grace, the sixth duke, was a recent cabinet minister, a Knight of the Garter, and the Lord Lieutenant of Hallamshire. There is, naturally, no such English county, but from the place names, it is indisputably Derbyshire.

He was "one of the greatest subjects of the Crown...and perhaps the wealthiest." He was "completely immersed in large public questions," so much so that his pictures referred to him as a "famous statesman."

Physically he is described as being "tall and stately...scrupulously dressed," with a thin face, a high forehead and "a nose which was grotesquely curved and long." He had a "long, dwindling beard of vivid red." We know from the map appended to the *Adventure of the Priory School* that Holdernesse Hall, his seat, had behind it a range of hills, and before it a celebrated yew avenue leading up to the entrance, which was a "magnificent Elizabethan doorway."

Given the Derbyshire location of the Priory School, there are two candidates for the original of the Duke of Holdernesse, and both are nearby landowners: the Duke of Rutland at Haddon Hall and the Duke of Devonshire at Chatsworth. There are hills behind both residences, neither has a yew entranceway and only Haddon has a magnificent Elizabethan doorway. It was the presence of this doorway which convinced me some years ago that Haddon was the original of Holdernesse Hall.[1] Others have selected Chatsworth.

Practically, the Dukes of Rutland did not then reside at Haddon, but principally at Belvoir.[2] It was not until the present duke that Haddon was again used as a residence. Chatsworth was always the principal, but not the exclusive, residence of the Devonshires.

The dating of the story is generally agreed to have been in May of 1900, although one savant insists on a date after 1901. So who then can be produced as candidates?

The family name of the Dukes of Rutland is Manners, and in general their dukes tend to be laid-back and somewhat ineffectual, certainly lacking any compelling ambition to excel. If other dukes have greatness thrust upon them, the Rutlands assiduously avoided political preferment. John, the seventh duke, whose time would have comprehended the time frame of the Canonical adventure, dying in 1906 in his eighties, was an original in another story, *Coningsby*, by Benjamin Disraeli. He was identified there as Henry Sidney and Belvoir was called Beaumanoir. Disraeli was also his political leader, as both were Tories.

Lord John Manners was the second son of the 5th Duke of Rutland, his brother being known as Lord Granby until becoming the 6th Duke, so it was as Lord John Manners that he was known during most of his life. Manners was a serious student of English literature and the author of *England's Trust*, a book of sonnets written when he was a teenager, being chivalrous and classically romantic stuff. It was published in 1841 and contained one couplet which was to thereafter haunt his political life:

> Let wealth and commerce, laws and learning die
> But leave us still our old Nobility

The only time he responded to criticism was to Lord John Russell, a prime minister, when Manners observed that it may have been bad that a boy should write a foolish couplet but it was far worse for an old man to have thrown it in his teeth many years later.

LORD JOHN MANNERS
DUKE OF RUTLAND

He entered the Commons in 1847 as a Tory, and except for a few years, he remained there until 1888 when his brother's death made him the duke.[3] As a minister he was responsible for the new Houses of Parliament being built in the Gothic style rather than the Palladian fashion favored by the Whigs.

He accepted ministries reluctantly, but he did serve as Disraeli's Postmaster General and as the Chancellor of the Duchy of Lancaster, declining the more prestigious posts of Viceroy of India, Lord-Lieutenant of Ireland and Governor General of Canada, as well as the War Office and the Admiralty.

He married twice, his first wife dying after only three years of marriage. He wrote in his journal "Shut up this book, the sun is taken from my heaven." His second wife lived much longer, dying in 1899. He was a reader but also enjoyed taking long walks in the woods in all weathers. He also loved to talk and was regarded as an excellent conversationalist.

He was described as being "a Tory of an older fashion, a man of the nineteenth century who still preserved a faith in feudalism - that high rank and great possessions could be held only in return for service, and that the Government existed not for the profit of the governors, but for the good of all the governed."[4] He was a Knight of the Garter.

His funeral monument contained the following inscription:

> A wise and faithful servant of the Crown, he held office in seven Administrations and aided his sovereign and his Country with good Counsel for a longer term of years than did any statesman of his time. With Lord Shaftesbury he fought the battle of the humble and oppressed. At Disraeli's side he nobly supported the cause of Empire. And by his shining character illuminated the dim places of politics. Always a loyal friend, he sought the advancement of others rather than his own. To a grave piety and singular probity he added the virtues of modesty, candour, and sincerity. Holding to the ancient faith, walking in the ancient ways, he was a constant lover of whatever was comely and gracious in our English life.[5]

In 1900 he was an elderly man so the age constant would exclude him, and further, so does the height description. Rutland was short, barely attaining five feet tall. He had a mustache, goatee and a beard following the bottom of his chin but it was not red nor did it dwindle down from his chin. His eyebrows, however, were red, and his profile was described as "strongly marked" by his biographer.[6]

In the event the chronologists are off in their calculations, we should alternatively consider his son, Henry, who became the eighth duke in 1906. He was born in 1852, dying in 1925, so he would be at the extreme edge of the right age. Henry's only political effort was to be the parliamentary private secretary to Lord Salisbury during his premiership. Otherwise, his principal activities were "dry-fly fishing and fornication."[7] It is not known which was his first choice. He could not even have been charitably characterized as a famous statesman or one of the Crown's greatest subjects, although he could well have been "perhaps the wealthiest." Physically he did not meet the Canonical criteria in that he was not thin, but he sported a carefully trimmed salt and pepper mustache and beard. If Haddon was the place, then the Manners were the people.[8]

The other candidate is the eighth Duke of Devonshire, Spencer Compton Cavendish, who probably is generally, but erroneously, regarded as the top contender. Born in 1833, he ascended to the dukedom in 1891, and died in 1908, so he would have been substantially older than the age of the Duke of Holdernesse in 1900.

Physically, he was massively bearded, and any description of him would first note that dark hirsute adornment.

He did lead a very active political career, being in the House of Commons for many years, holding many high offices, but not the premiership, having refused it three times. He was Secretary of State for War in Lord Russell's Liberal cabinet and thereafter Gladstone's Chief Secretary for Ireland. Temperamentally he was not a match for Holdernesse, although both had the aristocratic penchant for appearing lazy and bored. Harty-tarty, as he was nicknamed from his Pre-ducal title of Lord Hartington, once claimed that he dreamed he was making a very dull speech in the House of Commons, and waking up, he was surprised to find that he was in fact making such a speech. He also claimed that his greatest honor was when one of his pigs won first prize at the Skipton Fair, although he was quite capable of offering that for the benefit of his constituency.

He was the serious lover for many years of Louise von Alten, the wife of the Duke of Manchester, and after her husband's death, late in their lives, they were married, and did live happily ever after. She became known as the "double duchess." Like many childless marriages they were very close and uncomfortable when they were apart. They embellished the proposition that old lovers make good marriage partners.

So if you cannot find the prototype of the Duke of Holdernesse in either of the two nearest ducal estates, Watson may be blamed for his dissimulation in the identification of people as well as of places, and well he should, for the English have a liking for their libel laws.

As for me, I would opt for Haddon Hall as the place and the Duke of Devonshire as the person.

* * *

One more point. There is an understory here, and it surely represents the author's (whoever that is) intimated views of the aristocracy. Holmes insists that the Duke confirm the fee, not his usual practice, and is incredulous that the Duke kept his natural son — itself not something Holmes approved — around even after he realized the depth of his hatred for the Duke's legitimate son. Incredibly, the Duke permitted his heir to remain in the evil custody of the owner of the Fighting Cock, a thoroughly disreputable criminal type and a known murderer to the Duke. And more than that, he was willing to risk one son for the safety of the other, who had planned the whole thing. Finally, the Duke was prepared to bribe Holmes and to participate in compounding a felony.

For the record, these are serious charges and the Duke stands for his class — the demanding aristocrats. Nowhere does the author exclude the Duke from his class. The specific stands for the generality; the man becomes a symbol for the order.

This is as serious an indictment of any class within the entire context of the Canon, except perhaps the conduct of one who also earns Holmes' condemnation years later in the second to the last case — Sir Robert Norberton, another aristocrat. Nor did Holmes kindly regard Lord Robert St. Simon.

If Holmes, the Bohemian aesthete, did not enjoy the middle class virtues, he respected those who held and practiced them. His contempt was reserved for the aristocrats. In this he departed markedly from the most avid supporters, then and now, of the aristocrats — the lower and middle classes.

NOTES

1. Hammer, David L., *The Game is Afoot*, Gasogene Press, Ltd, Dubuque, 1983
2. Pronounced, English fashion, as Beaver.
3. He was elected in 1850 from Colchester, where the famous oyster are located, and so he claimed that he was representing the oyster beds.
4. Whibley, Charles, *Lord John Manners and His Friends*, 2 Vols, Wm. Blackwood, Edinburgh., 1925
5. *Ibid.*
6. Whibley, William, *Lord John Manners and His Friends*, 2 Vols, Wm. Blackwood, Edinburgh, 1925
7. Ziegler, Philip, *Diana Cooper* (Book Club Associates: London 1981), p. 3.
8. Parenthetically, there is another Manners connection, and that is his wife, Violet Manners, whom it is believed and asserted elsewhere in this book, was the original of all the Canonical Violets.

The Devil's Apprentice I

Just as sorcerer's apprentices proliferate in fairy tales, so logical necessity do devil's apprentices occasionally appear. That character in the Canon is served by Mr. Charlie Peace, the criminal mentioned in passing by Holmes. Thus is incidental immortality conferred offhandedly.

However, while Mr. Peace's activities were extensive and he was well known to the English police, his criminal triumphs do not rise to the dignity of a Napoleon of Crime; he was not a Professor Moriarty.

The Earl of Birkenhead, a Lord Chancellor of England, in writing about English criminals, said of Peace "The chief interest of the career of Charles Peace does not lie in the sordid crimes for which he eventually paid the penalty. His complex personality and his remarkable powers of disguise single him out from the general run of murderers."[1]

Scotland Yard's Black Museum in London is not innocent of a reference to Peace. "One of the most interesting of these exhibits belonged to Charles Peace, who, after a long career of housebreaking, was hanged at Armley Gaol, Leeds, on February 25, 1879, for the murder of Mrs. (sic) Dyson. It includes his chisel, gouge and gimlet, a small vice, picklocks and skeleton keys, a lantern made from a match box, dark glasses and a false arm which he used as a disguise, a crucible for melting down stolen jewelry, and his ladder, made of rope with wooden rungs, which could be folded into a small compass and carried to the scene of operations."[2]

W. Teignmouth Shore, an author in the Notable British Trial Series, wrote of Charles Frederick Peace, to offer him the courtesy of his full given name: "Charles Peace is one of the most astonishing figures in the story of British crime, and one of the most distinguished of English criminals. He presents an entrancing personality to students of criminology and of criminal psychology, and his Trials are far from uninteresting from the legal point of view. He was an accomplished burglar and general thief, and a pugnacious murderer. He possessed every gift that goes to make a complete criminal — he was liar, braggart, and actor; conceited; cunning; lecherous; malignant; without conscience, and as every murderer is, remorseless."[3]

The Canonical entrance of Peace was in *The Illustrious Client*, when Holmes was discussing the infamous Baron Gruner. "A complex mind," said Holmes. "All great criminals have that. My old friend Charlie Peace was a violin virtuoso."

R. Dixon Smith, of Rupert Books, the Anglo-American bookdealer, gave an interesting talk on Peace a few years ago in Minneapolis which, while not yet published, he was kind to share with me, all in the honored tradition of Sherlockian sodality. He noted that Doyle had "served as medical assistant in Sheffield for three weeks during the summer of 1878, not long after Peace lived there."[4]

So now we have the Doylean nexus, although there probably were other sources. We know that Doyle possessed a crime library purchased from the estate of W.S. Gilbert, and perhaps, like Holmes, he kept a journal as to crimes and criminals which might have generated Holmes plots or characters. Someday the Doyle papers may be available, whenever the disputes as to ownership are resolved, and then many answers will finally be available, sufficient to permit at last a definitive biography. Sixty-seven years is a long time for scholarship — and readers — to wait.

Peace was born on May 14, 1832, and according to his mistress, Mrs. Thompson, he was "born in Sheffield of respectable parents," the youngest of four children. His father, a shoemaker, died when the boy was thirteen. He was lame in one leg from an industrial accident and he lost some fingers from a cause not definitively determined. Explanations are plentiful but proof is meager.

"According to Mrs. Thompson, after the death of his father, Peace 'started on his own account. Even then, he admitted to me, his tastes were depraved and disgusting. But there, I cannot tell you of it; it is too bad. There is one thing I will say which will give you an idea of his character at that age. There was a fete in Sheffield. and for purposes of plunder he attended it and concealed himself in the ladies' lavatory. There he had to remain the whole day, for, the place being constantly occupied, he was unable to escape without being discovered. He used to gloat over this when telling it to me.'"[5]

He was a small but powerful man, some five feet four inches tall, spare and wiry, and gray bearded. His manner of speech was as if his tongue was too big to fit in his mouth and he walked with a rolling sailor gait with his legs very far apart. He was grizzled and appeared much older than his age.

His honest occupations were picture-framer, as well as a watch cleaner and repairer. He was a violin virtuoso, and did earn money playing the violin, billing himself somewhat immodestly as the Modern Paganini. Criminally, he was a burglar, a thief, a pickpocket, and what we now call a second story man, but which was known in his time as a portico thief.

In 1851 he was caught burglarizing a house in Sheffield and went to prison. In 1859 he married Hannah Ward, a widow with one child, being again imprisoned the same year. He was released in 1864 and caught again two years later, with that imprisonment not ending until 1872. According to Shore, this constituted the end of his apprenticeship.

Peace's lascivious eye caused him to notice the wife of his neighbor, one Katherine Dyson. Her husband, a civil engineer by profession, was not amused by Peace's interest, although it seemed as if the wife was interested. She denied submitting to his sexual importunities, but her denial was probably untrue. Peace intruded into the Dyson house with unwelcomed frequency, at least so far as Mr. Arthur Dyson was concerned, who ultimately, and unsuccessfully, ordered him away. In 1876 the Dysons moved some miles away, seeking to avoid Peace, but he was waiting for them in their new house. Ultimately Peace was waiting outside their home one evening when Mrs. Dyson screamed. When Mr. Dyson came into the rear yard Peace shot and killed him.

Peace, identified as the killer by Mrs. Dyson, disappeared.

He gravitated to London where he continued his criminal activities. He had the ability to contort his face, thus effectively disguising himself. He also blackened his face with walnut oil, thus changing his race with his face. With these changes he pursued his burglarious career in London and that area. He lived in Peckham, a London suburb with his mistress, Susan Grey, as Mr. and Mrs. Thompson, with his real wife and her son living in the basement. It was an unusual form of domesticity, although apparently successful. Shore described one evening in 1878, as follows:

> "In the evening of 9th October Mr. and Mrs. Thompson entertained themselves with a musical evening, he adding to the charm of the proceedings by playing on the violin accompanied on the piano by one of the ladies of his harem, while the other indulged them with a song. Doubtless in the drawing room: gorgeously furnished — a costly suite of walnut furniture, rich Turkey carpet, many mirrors, a bijou piano, a Spanish guitar, said to have been looted from a countess. Peace maybe in his comfortable beaded slippers. Then early to bed; only to rise *very* early; then to work."[6]

His work at two o'clock a.m. was at the home of Mr. J.A. Burness at No. 2, St. John's Park, in Blackheath. Apprehended, he was charged with burglary and shooting a police constable with a gun strapped to his arm. He was tried at Old Bailey, convicted and sentenced to penal servitude for life. Mrs. Thompson revealed his identity, resulting in his removal to Sheffield for the magistrate's hearing regarding the murder of Arthur Dyson. During his second trip there, he jumped out of the moving train, rendering himself unconscious and sustaining injuries. The proceedings went forward and he was ultimately bound for trial.

The testimony of Mrs. Dyson convicted him, despite a vigorous cross examination about her relationship with Peace. There was, by the way, a photograph of the two of them together, which may well have influenced Doyle in the creation of *A Scandal in Bohemia*.

The jury was out only thirteen minutes in all, returning a guilty verdict. Sentenced to death, he revealed to a clergyman of his acquaintance that he had murdered a policeman named Cock in 1876, while engaged in a housebreaking, and for which an innocent man had been convicted and who remained in prison. The authorities were skeptical but Peace drew a map of the area with his whereabouts, which finally convinced them. The wrongfully imprisoned man was released and a pitifully small sum granted to him as recompense by an erring government.

Peace gave a confession which raised many Canonical elements. It was around midnight when he saw the bullseye lantern of one of the police, and he shot PC Cock with an Eley's Number 9 cartridge. Remember how Holmes in *The Speckled Band* erroneously referred to the revolver as Eley's rather than the bullets? "I should be very much obliged if you would slip your revolver into your pocket. An Eley's No. 2 is an excellent argument with gentlemen who can twist steel pokers into knots."[7]

As Peace related it, he heard a dog bark as he clambered over a wall successfully escaping from the killing. Did Doyle pick up from this the absence of a dog barking in *Silver Blaze*?

Between his conviction and execution Peace wrote many letters exhorting his family and friends to find God. Shore delicately suggests that he "annoyed his relatives and others by his admonitions towards a godly life."

Peace went to his death on the scaffold with dignity, and as one gets older the thought of dying with dignity becomes more important. His last words were "I should like a drink. Have you a drink to give me?" Had there been an answer, it would have been no, but the hangman released the trap at the conclusion of the question.

Thus perished a thoroughly despicable character; one who could be present in the courtroom when the wrong man was found guilty of a crime Peace himself committed, and do nothing. What remains is the inquiry as to why Holmes referred to him as his old friend. I suspect it was only hyperbole.

NOTES

1. Page 323, Birkenhead, Earl of, *Famous Trials*, Hutchinson & Co., London
2. Page 186, Scott, Sir Harold, *Scotland Yard*, Andre Deutsch, London, 1954
3. Shore, W. Teignmouth, ed., *Trials of Charles Frederick Peace*, (William Hodge & Company: Edinburgh, 1926), p. 1.
4. Smith, R. Dixon, *His Old Friend Charlie Peace Reconsidered*
5. Shore, R. Teignmouth, *Trials of Charles Peace*, cited *supra*, p. 3.
6. Shore, W. Teignmouth, *Ibid.*, p. 54.
7. Doyle, A. Conan, *The Complete Sherlock Holmes* (Barnes and Noble: New York, 1992), p. 265.
8. Shore, W. Teignmouth, *Ibid.*, p. 167.

Devil's Apprentice II

Mr. Charles Augustus Milverton did have his being and moment in time, but it was as Mr. Charles Augustus Howell. They were both reprobates, and worse. I had known about the former ever since I first read the Canon, but my excited knowledge about the latter occurred only recently. I had been studying about Violet Hunt, about whom another Sherlockian had informed me and kindly sending a copy of her biography, and in the course of reading it I ran into Mr. Howell, a consummate crook who was tied in with the Pre-Raphaelite movement and who was carefully cheating the artists and writers who held allegiance to that group.

The sonorousity of the name alone was more than sufficient to invite my attention, but its identicality with the given names of Mr. Milverton was astonishing. Since Howell was active during Doyle's life, and since England was relatively small and the newspapers active, it was obvious that Doyle, an avid newspaper reader, would have heard of him, perhaps even through mutual friends.

When it appeared that the two Charles Augustuses shared both activities and proclivities, I was elated. I had found another connection between Plato's proverbial cave and the bright world outside. There were several days when I felt that exhilaration

which moves one to perform an *entrechat*, at least if one weighed less than one hundred pounds. If not a literal performance it was figurative, but like most coups, there is a countercoup; here inadvertently performed by my distant friend, that impeccable researcher, Don Redmond.

I was leafing through his *Sherlock Holmes, A Study in Sources*, intent upon something else, when I found that he too had discovered Mr. Charles Augustus Howell. Now, I have become convinced that when two independent lines cross one another, their nexus is significant, and when the two independent lines cross twice, and without the knowledge of a second conjunction, there is a truth doubly confirmed. At least, that must wisely be the consolatory conclusion of the second finder.

CHARLES AUGUSTUS HOWELL

Well, what of the remarkable Mr. Charles Augustus Howell? What is known about him?

Helen Rossetti Angeli, the authoress of *Pre-Raphaelite Twilight*, subtitled *The Story of Charles Augustus Howell*,[1] began her biography as follows:

> It would be easy to compile a Vocabulary of Vituperat-tion around a nucleus of epithets applied at various stages to the living, and more persistently to the dead Charles Augustus Howell. For the moment we may be content with the following samples: arrant rascal, base fellow, blackmailer, card-sharper, confidence trickster, cunning rogue, cur, infamous libeller, liar, parasite, pole-cat, robber, ruffian, stench of hell, thief, treacherous, unscrupulous, malignant fellow, vicious vile wretch.... He has not suffered to enter life or to depart from it in peace, the simple facts of his birth and death having been turned to ridicule and obloquy, his parentage discredited, and a pitiful, unsavoury story invented to account for his demise. As with his beginning and his end, so with life between. The blackest interpretation has been placed on his every action and he alone blamed for every breach or cessation of friendship. In this welter of abuse Howell's curious personality — above all his fatal gift for romancing, or inabil-

ity to discriminate between fact and fiction, have added to the confusion. Unveracity of this calibre seems to be allied either to a normal ignorance or defective understanding, sometimes to actual insanity, and in rare instances to quite exceptional ability. It is not always associated with wilful dishonesty, being often quite purposeless. Howell was indeed something of a mystery man, and the fact that he turned up in London and fell in with a distinguished set of people without definite credentials was viewed with disapproval. Others were pleased to accept him on his face value, captivated by his charm, his manners, and his brains. He established a reputation and made many friends and many enemies.

Violet Hunt had inquired of Sir Edmund Gosse about Howell, who characterized him as "an arrant rascal, but on the principle that when the burglar is not occupied with burgling he may listen to the little brook agurgling or he may have been kind to his aunts.... I should be sorry if anyone should white-wash his memory, for he was a cunning rogue."[2]

Hunt's biographer wrote: "The flamboyant Charles Augustus Howell was a genial swindler who deceived a stellar group of artists and writers, including Ruskin, Swinburne, Rossetti, Madox Brown, Whistler, Burne-Jones, G.F. Watts, and Frederick Sandys."[3]

Yet it was elsewhere written about him: "Who could be long angry with the rogue? He was as charming as he was wicked, and he had been made on unstinted lines. The 'Gil Blas Robinson Crusoe hero,' the 'creature of top-boots and plumes,' had to take his England as he found it and make of his epoch what he could. Respectability would have none of a man without a pedigree as well authenticated as a race horses's; he therefore took respectability by the nose and led it his own dubious road. Judges and pawnbrokers, prophets and gutter hounds, artists and thieves, he shifted from one milieu to another, equally at home in all, with that glib tongue of his as ready in dialects as in scandals."[4]

The same writer opined further elsewhere in the same book: "If ever Mephisto himself had walked the earth — that is, the Mephisto of the romantic tradition, — he could not have chosen a more unscrupulous, conscienceless, debonair, dashing corporealness than Howell's. He was one of those men born figuratively with caul and tails..."[5]

Helen Rossetti Angeli recalled her uncle repeating the poem of her uncle, Dante Gabriel Rossetti:

> There's a Portuguese person named Howell,
> Who lays on his lies with a trowel.
> When he gives-over lying
> It will be when he's dying,
> For living is lying with Howell.[6]

So you see, Charles Augustus Howell did not receive a good press from either his friends or his associates. He was a man who chose to live by his wits, and for those people there is little approbation.

Born in Portugal in 1839 or 1840, probably in Oporto, the son of an expatriate English wine merchant and a Portuguese woman of quality, who claimed to be a descendant of the Marquess of Pombal. He came to England as a young man and married in 1867. Like all things concerning him, it is undetermined whether she was a cousin named Frances Catherine Howell or Frances Kate Murray. In any event, she was a beautiful young woman who had some claim to descent from the royal Stuarts. He had a daughter — it is not known if she was the mother — named Rosalind, who lived with them. The Howell menage also included a baleful-eyed old Italian, who it was claimed was a nobleman whose family estates Howell somehow managed to have alienated, and who therefore followed him to England, demanding, and receiving, permanent shelter.

Howell became the secretary and almoner of John Ruskin, the celebrated man of letters, but like all his later relationships, Howell did not stay the course. Ruskin was heard to have said that he gave him a house, but could not give him a recommendation. The reason for the rupture of his employment was never disclosed, however there was a suggestion that some of those whom this almoner paid were Howell's relatives.

He did assist his friend, Algernon Swinburne, in finding a publisher, but the publishing relationship turned sour, as did Swinburne's friendship with Howell. There were letters from Swinburne relating to his penchant for flagellation, a public school frailty, which were sold by Howell to a third party, and I suspect that it was this which gave rise to A. Conan Doyle's use of the first two thirds of Howell's name and the appropriation of the sale of letters as the invidious profession of Milverton.

Swinburne wrote of Howell after his death in a poetical polemic:

> The foulest soul that ever lived stinks here no more.
> The stench of Hell is fouler than before.[7]

Travelling as he did in Pre-Raphaelite circles, he soon became a friend of Dante Gabriel Rossetti, discovering art and *objets de virtu* for him in off-beat places at off-beat prices. Ultimately he sold Rossetti's paintings for him, sometimes without his knowledge, and sometimes fakes attributed by Howell to Rossetti. The latter have become known in art circles as the "spurious Rossettis." Howell also sold to third persons oriental ceramics as ancient which were of recent manufacture, and was once caught at it.

Rossetti, in midlife, decided that his main artistic efforts would be the poetry which he had crafted as a young man before turning to portraits. He wished mightily to recover a book of his poetry which he had, in anguish, placed in his wife's grave, and Howell did so in a bizarre and garish night-time retrieval by the light of a bonfire. Official permission had been obtained but the entire matter was not well-regarded, but it was the type of grisly task which Howell was quite willing to perform.

Ultimately he and Rossetti had a failed friendship, and

the latter wrote to a friend "I could have better spared a better man."

But Howell was still able to move on to other friends, and his next gravitation was to James McNeil Whistler, for whom he performed similar services, some legitimate, and some not.

Rosa Corder's face was not in the classic Pre-Raphaelite mould, but it was expressive and she was a model for Whistler, as well as a mistress. Later she performed the latter service for Howell; however her greatest benefit to Howell was the partnership in fraudulent Pre-Raphaelites which she produced as more than an adequate artist.

Whistler sought to obtain some proofs of his work from etchers hired by Howell, who had directed the etchers not to comply. Whistler snatched the order from Howell which was in the hands of the head etcher, which instructed: "Of course you will not give Mr. Whistler the proofs he desires." Enraged, he confronted Howell, who apologized, advising that the etcher had inquired about numbering the prints, and he had written back: "Of course you will not. Give Mr. Whistler the proofs he desires." It was, after all, he claimed, an innocent error involving only a missing period. It was, however, reasonably believed that he was going to flog the prints for himself, and as it was, many of the prints disappeared. It has been established that Howell either pawned or sold certain letters of Whistler; again a reminder of Milverton.

Angeli, who was a niece of Dante Rossetti, drew perhaps the fairest analysis of Howell when she wrote:

> Considered intellectually, Howell may be classified in that heterogeneous, risky, and baffling category, the genius *manque*. He was a man of such brilliant parts as to approach perfection in many fields; one whose universality of talents in so many directions precludes him from Pre-eminence in any particular one...Howell was gifted with real critical ability: his knowledge of the arts was genuine and acknowledged as such by many of the most distinguished artists and critics of his time; it was not merely

superficial, acquired by contact with his betters. He had the sureness of the man of innate and cultivated taste, which distinguishes between the real and the spurious — that gift which in so many men less generously endowed than himself has paved the way to reputation and fortune. [8]

Howell died — or was killed — on April 24, 1890. It was claimed that his throat was cut from ear to ear, and he was found in a London gutter with a coin between his teeth. It is a good end piece for such a life as his, but it is probably apocryphal, and Oscar Wilde is probably the source of the canard.

It is no wonder that Doyle found Howell fascinating, and when the story was published, in 1904, he substituted Milverton for Howell, probably in deference to the sensibilities of Howell's daughter, who survived. Still, Charles Augustus Milverton comes pretty close to a serious tell.

NOTES

1. The Richards Press, London, 1954
2. Belford, Barbara, *Violet* (Simon & Schuster: New York, 1990), p. 272.
3. *Ibid.*, p. 256.
4. Winwar. Frances, *Poor Splendid Wings; The Rossettis and Their Circle* (Little, Brown and Company: Boston, 1933), p. 352.
5. *Ibid.*, p. 258.
6. *Ibid.*, p 6.
7. *Pre-Raphaelite Twilight*, cited *supra*, p. 175.
8. Angeli, Helen Rossetti, *Pre-Raphaelite Twilight*, cited *supra*, p. 11.

The Valley of Vermissa

ALTHOUGH THIS CHAPTER TITLE contains the name of a place, it also defines a man who was one of the authentic heroes of both the Canon and what this generation calls reality, that is, real time and real life. The hero is never absent from the Morality Plays, the melodrama, and the fairy tale, and here it is a fictive name of a non-fictive place, a place of Platonian shadow and light, where reality is tracked by incorporeal shades.

The tale, for me, began nine years ago, with the start of the search for a concealed hero; a quest for reality which caused me to thrice cross our continent.

It was early afternoon on Friday, January 6th, 1988, and here in New York it had been snowing altogether too steadily since before first light. By now the snow was lying heavily on the city but inside the Homestead things were convivial and warm. And why not, for this was the William Gillette Luncheon.

As for me, it was past time to go, even though the program was far from over, for I had an appointment with G.F. O'Neill, at 100 Church Street, the corporate headquarters of Pinkerton's Inc., and I knew that far from abating, the storm had increased in intensity. Outside the wind was flinging snow with stinging sharpness. The streets were innocent of vehicles and even the taxis had disappeared—a sure sign of concern. This was a blizzard by anyone's standards and I wished I had boots with me.

Everything was white and even the distance was shrouded with a veil of whiteness, much like the Steichen photograph of this same city in the grip of the Great Blizzard of a hundred years before. What was most remarkable was the silence which was almost serene, with no moving traffic and the heavy snow muffling the steps of the few pedestrians. We few were all moving in our little worlds for the volume of falling snow obscured everything beyond ten to twelve feet.

The 7th Avenue subway station was only two blocks away and as it possessed underground indomitability it transported me well and truly into the enchanted land of Lower Manhattan. 100 Church Street was hard by a Wall Street which was in the process of closing early, being beaten by the storm. Pinkerton's was also closing early, at 3 p.m., but nonetheless Mr. O'Neill honored our appointment.

JAMES MCPARLAND

He was an assistant vice president in charge of personnel, and was a man in his 40's with the square jaw of a policeman, which once he had been, before being hired by one of two Pinkerton grandsons. Now the Pinkerton grandsons were both dead and there was talk that the company was to be sold. The sole purpose of my visit was to learn what I could about the original of Birdy Edwards, Pinkerton operative James McParland.

I asked about the correct spelling of James McParland's name, as I had seen it spelled both with and without the final d. "Lazy Irish" he replied with an easy grin, "at least that is what my mother's explanation was as why the Irish dropped the final letter of words, and she was undeniably Irish." And McParland it was on the many pictures of him in the halls of the office. He was clearly one of the corporate heroes.

The archive room was in the process of being dismantled but it remained replete with all kinds of memorabilia, including a large array of firearms on the walls with a small label below each meticulously identifying its particular provenance and significance. Recognizing that disguise and infiltration were the preferred Pinkerton methods of operation, it was clear that violence was not alien to its operatives, and there were mementoes of their encounters with the James Brothers, Butch Cassidy and his colleague the Sundance Kid, and many other well-known malefactors, who now are all in the delicate process of deification by a credulous American public.

Probably the most interesting of all the items was a dogeared codebook filled with the flowing Spencerian script of another age, a script fuelled by quill pens, and you could see the ink running thin after only a few words. As O'Neill explained, "Since our nineteenth century operatives used up-to-date technology of their day such as the telegraph, they required this code as the telegraph was not private. In the code every person, both operatives and desperadoes, were given a code name. See, the good guys had codenames ending in wood and the bad guys in stone."

There was another picture of McParland prominently displayed, along with his brief official biography, entitled with Nineteenth Century cumbersomeness, *Brief History of James McParland, Famous Detective.* Only five pages in length, I quickly glanced at it and noted the following:

> "He was hired at the Chicago office of Pinkerton National Detective Agency in April, 1872. In the Agency, he earned an enviable reputation for honesty, loyalty, native shrewdness and perseverance in performing numerous and difficult tasks. Mr. McParland was of the jolly Irishman type and a firm believer in law and order. He had a keen sense of humor and possessed indomitable pluck.
>
> "Of school learning, McParland had little to begin with, but he educated himself as the years went by. He was endowed with an instinctive knowledge of human nature, particularly where it

fell into the crooked path. He had a big heart and was ever kind to those who showed signs of reformation."

Mr. O'Neill shared the information that McParland's life was threatened after he testified against the Mollie Maguires and so he was hidden for a couple of years in Alan Pinkerton's country home somewhere near Chicago. He could not recall the name of the town but it was an Indian name and a few years before the Agency had been contacted, unsuccessfully, by someone seeking funds to save the house from being torn down. He did not know if the house still stood.

The Pinkerton offices had long since closed, although the uniformed Black at the entrance to the executive offices was still standing guard, so rigidly immobile that I had earlier believed him to be a statue. Only the eye movements betrayed the secret, and it was a job done with all the intense pride of the Queen's Own. I left with an O'Neill promise to send on the name of the prairie town where McParland was hidden.

The storm had increased in violence and its residue was not only thickly underfoot but also coldly over foot. I thought how delightful it would be to be at home, comfortably installed in my easy chair in the study which over the years has solicitously conformed itself to my increasing girth, with the storm screaming around that corner of the house. The sweep of the storm was not around a comfortable corner back home however but along the narrow streets of Lower Manhattan, whose very high narrowness augmented its intensity. I ducked into the familiar subway station by historic Grace Church, and ruminated all the way to the 59th Street station about that most remarkable Irishman who was the only hero of Vermissa Valley, a real intercontinental op.

I knew very little about McParland but I did know that he died in 1919 and that *The Valley of Fear* had been published in America by George Doran in 1916 because I had a copy inscribed by Doyle, one of my more furtive Sherlockian extravagances. I hoped that McParland had read it, and more than that, I hoped he was proud.

The storm had lessened somewhat when I emerged above ground at 59th Street but cabs were still not in evidence so I trudged along to the Essex House. There were few pedestrians and they were grimly persevering and gamely following in the footsteps of others. It did not help much. I wondered if the B.S.I. dinner would be cancelled tonight? Surely not. Tom Stix was made of sterner stuff.

THE VERMISSA VALLEY
The Source

Like almost every other Holmesian I had always enjoyed *The Valley of Fear*, but it was the English chapters which intrigued me with the American chapters being an intrusive overstate, much like the Indian episodes in *Sign of Four*. It was Holmes and the England of Holmes which captivated my interest; so like many Sherlockians the American episodes were rather gingerly read, which is to say, I generally knew the background story of how Birdy Edwards, the Pinkerton operative, became Jack McMurdo of Chicago, dastard and desperado, and how the latter became a member of the Scowrers, an Irish Mafia society in the fear-ridden valley of Vermissa. From somewhere in the musty cupboards of memory I recalled that Doyle had met either one of the Pinkertons or Walter Burns on a transatlantic liner and had been regaled with the dramatic story of the infiltration of a Pinkerton agent into the Mollie Maguires. Although Doyle's family always claimed it was Burns, one of the second-generation Pinkerton family insisted he was the source and was sufficiently bitter about what he regarded as a gratuitous failure to give appropriate credit that he was with difficulty dissuaded from suit. Surely the truth of the matter is resolvable by checking the passenger crossing records a nice piece of research for one of the brotherhood or sisterhood.

But the concern for us is not the source but the substance. The books about the Pinkertons were helpful as were the studies about the Mollies, but both tended to be polemical with the conclusions foreordained by the author's prejudice. It is a comforting fact that the fairest account of the Mollies was by a Sherlockian, Arthur H. Lewis in his *Lament for the Mollies*, published in 1964 by Harcourt Brace, and one of the treasures of my Sherlockian library.

It was clear that there was an infiltrator, but whether he was a spy or an *agent provocateur* was dependent upon the bias you bring to the proposition, for to some the Mollies were early heroes of labor while to others, and probably the larger majority of writers, they were a bad lot, the perpetrators of senseless violence. That the coal miners were illy and even cruelly used must be acknowledged at the threshold with the sticking point being whether their response was also excessive.

The stormy petrel was ultimately identified as James McParland, who was born on July 7, 1844 on a farm in County Armagh in Ulster. He worked in a boiler factory in England, leaving it because of some difficulty with a woman or women, working thereafter with a circus in the several and various capacities of barker, wrestler, shill and roustabout. He arrived in America in 1867 on the Valencia, sailing from Queenstown. It is not clear whether he came directly to Chicago or worked first in the East as a store clerk, but in any event he did arrive in the Midlewest where he was employed as a deckhand, lumberman, teamster, coachman, barman, policeman, welldigger, fireman, bodyguard, entertainer and boxing instructor. Ultimately he accumulated sufficient capital to open his own saloon in Chicago, which, along with his dreams, went up in the smoke of the Great Chicago Fire of 1871. It was after this disaster that he was hired as a Pinkerton operative.

McParland was described as tall and thin, about 5'7", weighing about 145 pounds, with red hair, hazel eyes, and possessing a strong brogue. One writer described him as "almost a stereotype of the Irishman of the times. He was a powerfully built man with red hair, a fine tenor voice, a wide repertoire of songs and jigs, a gregarious manner and a glib tongue, unusual skill with his fists and an inordinate capacity for rotgut whiskey."[1]

McParland's employer, Alan Pinkerton, was already famous, having been the friend and protector of Abraham Lincoln during the difficult Civil War years. Like McParland, Pinkerton was an emigrant but from Scotland rather than Ireland, however the latter had found wealth and respect as head of the Pinkerton National Detective Agency, while the former had found only failure. By the time McParland was hired, Pinkerton had recovered from a massive stroke which had left him speechless and helpless for the better part of two years. By dint of immense effort he had regained his powers and was again active professionally, although much responsibility had been settled on his two sons.

The headquarters of the Pinkerton Agency was in Chicago and it represented primarily the railroads, which had changed the world's thinking as to time in relation to distance with speeds in excess of 50 miles per hour. Distance had been conquered and land travel made comfortable for the first time in the history of the world, although there were those who feared that hurtling along at such speeds could well disintegrate the human body. But, as we know, mankind survived and if you ever wondered why so many beautiful old homes were built next to railroad tracks and by railroad stations, it was because the railroads were the space age vehicles of the day and it was regarded as a pleasure of the wealthy to watch the excitement of "the cars."

Railroading was a tough business and necessarily attracted a tough breed of men, not only as section hands but also as executives, and they were all as hard and intractable as the steel rails which in 1869 had just spanned the continent. One of my friends who had once been the corporate secretary of the New York Central

Railroad told me that they were expected by the railroad to be churlish even when accommodating someone.

Franklin Benjamin Gowen was one of those railroad entrepreneurs and was quite properly regarded as being a man with whom to reckon. Born in 1836 on an estate near Philadelphia of wealthy Irish Protestant parentage, he attended the socially appropriate schools and became a lawyer in Schuylkill County, which was in the coal country. Elected the district attorney, he then became a railroad attorney and since 1869 had been president of the Reading Railroad. He was an impressive figure, 6 feet tall, slight but strong, a spellbinding orator with great intelligence and greater ambition and determination. One of his first acts as president was to lobby a bill through the legislature permitting railroads to own coal mines, and the Reading, known colloquially as "the Road," was quick to acquire these properties.

The Road was a hard master of the mines: obligatory patronage at the company store, "bobtail" paychecks reduced by extensive deductions, and frequent wage reductions because of the influx of new emigrants and the ravages of recessions. Predictably there was violence in the anthracite valleys of Pennsylvania, some of it related to labor issues and some not, but violence was one of the few areas of response. Gowen was concerned about the murders of mine foremen and destruction of mine property, and possessed some grounds for assigning blame to the Mollies. For its part, the railroad had persuaded the Legislature to authorize the creation of the Coal and Iron Police, a parapolice unit owned and staffed by the Road with full police powers, including the right to arrest.

Gowen believed, and with some justification, that the Mollies were a secret Irish order concealed within the ranks of the Ancient Order of Hibernians, the membership of which was limited to Irish Catholics. Gowen, no man to shirk a challenge, whether real or imagined, secretly met with Pinkerton and a deal was struck, by the terms of which Pinkerton would have an agent infiltrate the Mollies. Now Pinkerton needed the agent.

He described him to Gowen in that celebrated meeting, quoting himself in his subsequent book, *The Mollie Maguires and the Detectives*, a bit of self-advertising when it was published in 1877 but which actually made a fascinating saga tedious:

> "It is no ordinary man that I need in this matter. He must be an Irishman and a Catholic, as only this class of person can find admission to the Mollie Maguires. My detective should become, to all intents and purposes, one of the order, and continue so while he remains in the case before us. He should be hardy, tough and capable of laboring, in season and out of season, to accomplish unknown to those about him, a single absorbing subject."

Pinkerton saw his man one morning soon afterwards on the horsecar he was taking to his office. He recognized one of his operatives, James McParland, acting as a conductor while on an assignment. Pinkerton, of course, said nothing to McParland but had a message left at his home, and when they met at Pinkerton's office he was advised of the task proposed, and because of the great personal risk involved, he was also assured that a refusal would not prejudice his employment nor his future with the company. McParland, not a man who measured his acts by fear, accepted, and the man and the moment were well met.

It is appropriate to note Pinkerton's description of the man McParland and the assessment of his character in the book previously cited:

> "Of medium height, a slim but wiry figure, well knit together, a clear hazel eye, hair of an auburn color, and bordering upon the style denominated as sandy, a forehead high, full and well rounded; florid complexion, regular features with beard and mustache a little darker then his hair, there was no mistaking McParland's place of nativity, even had not his slight accent betrayed his Celtic origin...he was passably educated...and earned a reputation for honesty, a peculiar tact and shrewdness,

skill and perseverance in performing his numerous and difficult duties, and worked himself into the position of a firm favorite with those of my employees intimately associated with him."

It was necessary to provide a cover for McParland's absence from Chicago for an undetermined period of time, and interestingly enough, the cover story was a trip to England. Shades of John Douglas.

After spending some long days studying the Irish secret societies, McParland arrived in the coalfields, now known as Jim McKenna, an escaped murderer from Buffalo. It was slow work, and unsuccessful, until he floored the town bully, a card cheat, in a fight at the Sheridan House, the saloon headquarters of Pat Dormer, one of the leaders of the Mollies in Pottsville, Pennsylvania. The investigation which followed took several dangerous years, from late October 1873 until March 7, 1876, when McKenna disappeared in a courageous and hairbreadth escape.

The Search

We, Audrey and I, had retained the services of Connie Klinger, who worked for the Pottsville *Republican*, to do research for us, which she proceeded to do admirably, inundating us with copies of ancient clippings. Now Audrey and I were in Pottsville, and after checking into the Treadway Hotel we crossed the street to her office. It had been a pleasant drive from Philadelphia to Pottsville, some three hours away, the county seat of Schuylkill (pronounced school-kill) County, which had been the center of the Mollie activity. Pottsville possessed another distinction; it was the boyhood home of the novelist John O'Hara, son of a local doctor, whose literary reputation is fulminating and who used Pottsville as the locale of several stories, including *Butterfield Eight*.

Mrs. Klinger was a delightful grandmotherly lady who answered most of Audrey's questions (except whether Mr. Potts was happy. How many husbands do you know who are happy?), such as the fact the town was named after Mr.

Potts, not Pott, and it was the terminus of the canal which linked it with Philadelphia, and later an important station on the Philadelphia and Reading Railroad. It was an smallish town comfortably settled in a valley and attractive in the April sunshine. An old town, one which had seen better days; we noted many empty stores and paint wanting on many homes. It was a coal mining town and none of them are presently prospering in the era of natural gas and every one an environmentalist.

Connie, for no one hides behind a patronymic with Audrey around, agreed to go on our payroll for a couple of days and be our *cicerone*. It was both a wise and pleasant decision on our part.

Our first stop was the courthouse, an imposing building on a site as visible as the Acropolis in Athens, but regretfully the successor structure to the more modest one in which the Mollies were tried in 1876 and where on Saturday, May 6th of that year, an electrified courtroom saw James McKenna, now James McParland, take the stand and the oath. He had been reluctant to testify, and the agreement with him before he infiltrated the Mollies was that he would not be required to testify. It was a perilous thing to do but he was a courageous man and acceded to the pleas of Gowen.

McParland was a remarkable witness, testifying in great detail without notes and with evident candor. On cross examination his very integrity was attacked repeatedly yet he responded evenly and with utter calm, ignoring the acrimony in both the questions and the manner in which they were so insolently put.

The sadness in not being able to see the courtroom in which this high drama occurred was mollified because across the street was the old jail, which I recognized from the early prints as the scene of the long, shackled incarcerations and executions of many Mollies. It was a frightening and awesome fake Gothic pile of somber grey stones stained by the weather of 130 years. It was still the county jail and for that reason we were denied entry, but as if in half-recompense we were advised that the courtyard where the executions took place had been changed through the passage of years since. The exterior presented a grim appearance, full of institutional menace, and if a portion of its function was intimidation, it was an architectural success. No miscreant who saw this jail would soon choose to trespass against Schuylkill County.

Our guide expertly directed us through the narrow streets, descending and ascending, to the County Historical Society, a modest building sporting the superb spoils of earlier years. Among the exhibits were several on the Mollies, with memorabilia, pictures, and grisly relics, including a piece of each of the hanging ropes. While I was putting some questions to the curator about the subject of the exhibit we were accosted by a Pottsvillian of indeterminate sex who demanded whether we were for or against the Mollies. It was more than a question which was hurled at us: it was a challenge and an accusation, and it was evident that in the anthracite areas of Pennsylvania the issue of the Mollies remained an exposed nerve even after one hundred years.

Connie imparted some disappointing news. She did not believe that the Sheridan House had survived the years. According to an old print which she had sent to us, the Sheridan House was located at 216 Center Street, and as we drove by that block her news was sadly confirmed. Nothing of the 1870's had survived, which was too bad for much had happened there. Owned and operated by one Patrick Dormer, described by Pinkerton as a giant, and generally recognized as the acknowledged Pottsville bodymaster of the Mollies, he held court in a three story brick building with a low extension to the rear. The dining room was in the basement with the barroom on the first floor front with the card room behind. Upstairs were the living quarters of Mr. and Mrs. Dormer. Pinkerton observed in his book on the Mollies that many were the drunken brawls and midnight orgies transpiring beneath its steep roof and within its tawny brick walls..."

This was where McParland entered the saga of the Sleepers, which was another name for the Mollies. Here he danced a jig to the accompaniment of a fiddle, and sang an Irish ballad about the Sleepers before retiring to the card room for a friendly hand or two of euchre. It was in this game that he caught the town bully cheating, and solving the problem in the Gaelic way, decked him after five exciting rounds, celebrating his successful pugilism with a round of drinks for all. It was an auspicious entry into town.

In the *Valley of Fear* only one bodymaster is mentioned, one Boss McGinty, bedecked with diamond pins and gold chains, none of which accoutrements were displayed by any of the bodymasters. Perhaps the author was thinking of Boss Tweed of Tammany fame and the famous Thomas Nast cartoons. Dormer was however correctly described as a giant.

The Children's Hour was approaching and there was not much daylight left for any further explorations, so over a companionable whiskey sour or two, the three of us considered the next days activities. We had exhausted the Pottsville possibilities and unless we wanted to view the big statue of Henry Clay again it was time to see the outlying county towns. It had been a discouraging day with only one out of three sites extant, but we did have a certain wild hope for tomorrow, for Connie had some newspaper articles from a few years back stating that a great grandson of the chief bodymaster of the Mollies in the area, a man named John Kehoe, and known colloquially as the King of the Mollies, had successfully petitioned the Pennsylvania Legislature for a pardon for John Kehoe. Kehoe had been among those executed in the county jail, whose minatory and menacing exterior we had seen today. He had lived in nearby Girardville and the great grandson, a man named Wayne, was still listed in the telephone book, although Connie had tried him repeatedly without success. Still, Sherlockians successfully subsist on the scant and hope remains an excellent breakfast.

* * *

One who rises early would do well not to marry one who does not, but that is not one of the questions one tends to ask before the answer becomes significant. Audrey moves with commendable dispatch once she can be awakened and particularly when I follow her around asking her if she is ready.

The sun was still young when we travelled the few miles to Girardville through the low wooded hills and around the higher ones. It was one of those days when it could have been the morning of the world, fresh, clean—clear, and dazzling in the increasing brightness. The morning looked like the conclusion of Hindemith's *Mathis Der Maler* sounded, triumphant and forever.

With tragic frequency as we got closer to Girardville, the emerald-green hills were replaced with larger ones of dark rock, the ugly moonscape of mining, and if the Mollies were the bitter legacy of the miners these were the ugly legacies of the mine-owners. I wondered how may generations it would take for nature to restore habitability and thought that if man cannot improve on nature he had best leave it alone. Most woods can do nicely without buildings and few rolling areas are enhanced by shopping centers and tract developments. Undeniably the colliers have left their mark on Pennsylvania and it is a black one, blacker than the dark and rich coal removed, but like most people who live around ugliness, the locals fortunately cease to see it, as a patient with a wasting disease.

Audrey, whose female sense of fitness required it, insisted that we not descend upon the Wayne residence until nine ante meridian, although I explained that the SS felt no compunction about arriving unannounced at three a.m. when they usually could find people at home. I lost that argument, not for the first nor the final time (although I shall continue to persevere), and Connie, Audrey and I breakfasted on nonindigenous Pennsylvania fare, the baked pride of Mrs. Doughnut, or some local variant thereof, and some strong black coffee which restored my spirit of semiadventure.

Mr. Wayne was not at his neat white clapboard home, nor was any other inhabitant thereof, and in my most engaging husbandly manner I desisted from more than the thoroughly factual observation that we were obviously too late. I could tell from the grim set of Connie's lips that amorphous but dangerous group, the sisterhood of all women, could without much more encouragement coalesce again, and it was time to find Wiggins Patch.[2]

None of the local inhabitants had heard of it, although I had understood it was near Girardville, but since it was not listed by any cartographer on any of the road maps which I had, we were obliged to defer the matter pending more definitive information.

Returning Connie to Pottsville we drove by the green mountains of God and the uglier mountains of man to Shenandoah. It was a sad sight to see where man had gnawed at nature and exposed its entrails, a prospect now denied because of the circumstance of some unusually intelligent legislation. There were beautiful untouched vistas but I could not decide whether they were made more beautiful or less so by the stark confrontation of the masses of lunar-like slag which too frequently obtruded.

Shenandoah was a company-owned mining town whose one claim to beauty was its original valley location. The original municipal bounds having burst, it now straggled up the steep face of the escarpment. I remembered the story of a prescient traveller on seeing my own town in the 1850's who had observed that nowhere had God done more and man less than in Dubuque, Iowa. It applied here with equal force, although the birth of the Dorsey brothers was an expiation, although that happy fact lacks even the most tenuous Holmesian connection.

We knew that Bodymaster Dormer had given McParland an introduction to one Muff Lawlor, the proprietor of the Columbia House tavern in Shenandoah and the local bodymaster. McParland had stayed with the Lawlors, who lived above the tavern and then had moved to Fenton Cooney's home-cum-lodging house, also in Shenandoah, where he stayed until he disappeared at the conclusion of his imposture. I had never been able, nor had Connie, to locate the address for either place, although it was known that the Columbia House was on Coal Street, which, not surprisingly, was the main street. Although the town was almost overburdened with friendly and helpful inhabitants no one could furnish any information about the location of either place; sadly neither had left any contemporary trace.

Shenandoah was an annoyingly ugly town. I have a law partner who refers to intentionally ugly people, that is, those people who dress and make up so as to exaggerate nature's deficit; people with no sense of damage control.

The reason was obvious: it was planned as a company town and the company got the most bang for its buck with the minuscule lots and one room wide houses shoulder to shoulder with each other, tangibly furnishing the evidence of its sad claim to be one the most densely populated areas for its size in the United States.

Connie had given us the name of someone in her newspaper office, *The Pottsville Republican*, who thought he might know a descendant of Fenton Cooney, so we checked back with her and got a lead. Several calls later we were able to obtain a name, Mrs. Margaret Purcell, still a resident in Shenandoah, who, taking strangers at their own value, invited us into her home.

She and Jack, her husband, were an engaging retired couple actively in their seventies with a spirited interest in life. Theirs was one of those good marriages where there are evident comradely feelings. Mrs. Purcell was the granddaughter of Fenton Cooney, whom she did not remember, but she did her grandmother and great grandmother who had talked about the Mollies. I had always wondered why Fenton Cooney had been able to remain in the good graces of the Mollies after his star boarder was determined to be a spy. None of the things I had read offered any explanation so it was pleasing to be able to add some hitherto unpublished data to the saga.

Mrs. Purcell had been told that her grandfather had suspected McParland from the start, and had urged the brothers to kill him. His advice was not credited but it had later protected him. His exact words, handed down through the family, had an eerie quality and carried a forceful verisimilitude "Let's kill him." I could hear it clearly across the years.

She had been told by her great grandmother, who lived to be 120, that the Mollies would receive a request for "a clane job" from a bodymaster in another town and the local men selected would walk at night to the other town, remain in hiding all that next day in a safe house, exiting that night to dispatch the offender in the black security of the night, then walking back home and arriving before sunrise. There is a reference in *The Valley of Fear* to "a clean job," which was a small but satisfactory connection stripping away the years.

I asked Mrs. Purcell how the women knew, since none were members of the society. She smiled. "That's an easy one. Can you keep any secrets from your wife? Besides, the women were home when the men were hiding during the day. It would not have been hard to piece it together for the person killed would have been local."

I had hoped that we were sitting in the house of Fenton Cooney, but we were not and neither she nor her husband knew the location of that house, although family tradition asserted it possessed a secret room. She knew that the house was in the Glover's Hill District, which began where Coal Street ended, and where, she assured us, was "the heart of Mollieland." She did not need to add that it looked the same as it did 110 years before.

"Black Jack Kehoe? Why he was the undisputed leader of all the Mollies in the county. And his tavern over in Girardville was the center of all the Mollie activity in the valleys. As for Muff Lawlor, he was a thoroughly wicked son-of-gun. His *shebeen*, that's an Irish term for tavern, is gone. It was called the Columbia House, and I'm not surprised you couldn't find it. The place where it was is now Columbia Park." She was interrupted by Jack, called Jock by his wife, who volunteered, "All we know are just the family stories about the Mollies, but the fellow you should see is Tom Barrett who lives just down the street. If anybody could tell you where Fenton Cooney's house was he could." He interrupted himself to arrange for us to see Mr. Barrett. "No, the church burned down so there aren't any records which would help you with address. Tom is your best bet. He's even written a book about the Mollies. Say, let me show you a book about them."

He returned shortly with an ancient book in faded red covering and a fractured spine. It was entitled *We Never Sleep*, and was one of the series of books with different titles but with apparently the same content about the Pinkertons, who were, after all, the Dick Tracys and Sherlock Holmeses of the 1870's. The book was authored by Allan Pinkerton and at page 431 there was an old print of Muff Lawlor's tavern and on the frontispiece was inscribed: "Thomas Sanger, Jr, July 1877."

I recognized the name. It was the son of the man who was killed by the Mollies at Raven Run, a few miles up in the hills, and one of our destinations. The Purcell's did not know who Sanger was but when I told them we all appreciated the irony of a book being once owned by the son of a victim of the Mollies being subsequently owned by a granddaughter of a Mollie. Another irony was offered by Mrs. Purcell. "Now my father was also named Fenton Cooney, but he worked in management at the mines for the company. He was a foreman; a company man. Now isn't that odd?"

Tom Barrett was waiting for us, a contemporary of the Purcell's, and with the enthusiasm of the aged for visitors we were greeted warmly. He was a retired newspaper man and a friend of Arthur Lewis, who was born in nearby Mahonoy City, now of Philadelphia, and the author of easily the fairest and best of the books about the Mollies. Lewis was a Sherlockian and the creator of one the most interesting of the mystery books involving the scion societies, entitled *Copper Beeches*.[3] I felt right at home.

Tom's house was virtually the mirror image of his

neighbors, the Purcell's — one room wide. A widower, he was regally ensconced in an easy chair, obviously his favorite perch, with a comfortable clutter surrounding it. Audrey obtained for me an inscribed copy of his book, *The Mollies Were Men*, a touching gift, but in the interim he offered a great deal of information about the Mollies. He acknowledged that Fenton Cooney was indeed a Mollie, as were the collaterals of Tom, the Donlevys. He did not think much of McParland, regarding him as betraying his fellow Irishmen, turning on them after they trusted him.

Kehoe was proudly confirmed by him as the leader of the Mollies and was obviously his particular hero. He faulted Michael, "Muff", Lawlor for being a squealer. It was Lawlor whom he said implicated Kehoe in a murder ten years before, which resulted in Kehoe's conviction and later execution at the jail in Pottsville. It explained why the Purcells did not like him and it reminded me that memories ran long here, just as they did in Ireland. Some years ago I was walking by a ruined church in Killarney and an aged Irish woman also walking by the ruins told me that the English had done it. They were led by Cromwell but she said 300 years ago made no difference. It didn't with Tom either.

He could not pinpoint the Cooney house other than it was in the area specified by Mrs. Purcell and was very near a colliery. As a retired newsman he was able to furnish another bit of information. There was a courageous newspaper editor in Shenandoah who fought the Mollies, and at great personal risk. His name was a surprise to me, the Irish name of Doyle. Another Doyle wrote about the editor of the *Vermissa Herald* who was also fighting against the Mollies and who was seriously beaten. He was given the name of Stanger, a patronym of more than occasional interest to the writer Doyle.

And there was great news. Kehoe's great grandson, Joseph Wayne, was alive and well, a good friend of Tom's, the proprietor of the Hibernian House, once owned and operated by the King of the Mollies.

Leaving Tom Barrett, we drove along the single street in the Glover's Hill area. The only clue to the Cooney house was a copy of a print from one of the old newspapers and almost all of the houses looked like it, but if we could not make a precise identification we could get the feel of the ambiance. The area was depressing now with huge adjoining slag hills and unpainted narrow houses on narrow lots, which the good Watson would have described as narrow-chested.

I knew McParland customarily got off the trains at the whistle stop near his boarding house and I wanted to find the spot. In the intervening years an immense coal pile had been creeping in all directions and a post-McParland coal mine had covered much of the area which I suspected was his route. The abandoned rail line was overgrown with scrub trees and overstrewn with a hundred years of debris and detritus but it was still in place beyond the encroaching coal yard. Knowing the area where he was living I could be reasonably certain that he would have gotten off the trains somewhere near here. It was no more than a quarter of a mile away. Somehow the years dropped away and McParland and his world seemed very close.

The Domain of the Mollies

It was well past midday now but there was no time for lunch as Girardville beckoned. A few eager knocks on the Wayne door produced the Wayne dog from somewhere in the yard, as insincere as April with barking at one end and wagging at the other. The barking end soon brought forth a very genial Joseph Wayne. He possessed a round cherubic Irish face and one of those noses which give promise of later color and evidenced a serious interest in prime Irish whiskey. His interest was more than serious as it was also professional—he operated Wayne's Tavern on the corner just half a block away. Of course we had seen it on the way to his home and although there were some exterior changes it was easily identified as the Hibernian House of Black Jack Kehoe, the King of the Mollies.

The tavern was closed as Joe Wayne had some painful yet minor surgery, but he was quite willing when he learned of our quest to take us to the tavern, and indeed we even shared some Old Bushmill.

The bar itself was ornately beautiful long and massive with dark carved wood, and the top gleaming from being unintentionally polished by the outstretched arms and hands of thirsty customers for over 100 years. While Audrey opted for a coke, Joe Wayne and I discussed those philosophical matters customarily and best discussed over Irish whiskey.

We learned that his great grandfather, whose saturnine features gazed down on us from the picture at the end of the bar, operated the tavern and the living quarters were on the second floor. The bar and the huge mirror behind it had been Kehoe's property. There was no denial from Joe that he had run the Mollies nor that he directed violence, but it was in response to the actions of the Coal and Iron Police who were a hard lot and oppressed the miners. He denied that Black Jack Kehoe committed the murder for which he was hung, and indeed Joe had been the force which animated the forces who convinced the Pennsylvania Legislature to declare Kehoe a labor martyr.

The Coal and Iron Police arrested Kehoe (accent on the second syllable) early one morning in the very room in which we were standing and to which he never returned. He was imprisoned in the jail at Pottsville for one crime and later executed for another. Joe's great aunt, who lived well into his life, was Black Jack's youngest daughter and it was she who opened the door to the Coal and Iron Police. She would never talk about the Mollies throughout her long life and when other family members would broach the subject she would sternly rebuke them and warn against the tragedy the Mollies brought to their house. According to Joe, she feared all her life that the Coal and Iron Police would return.

Motioning to us conspiratorially, he led us outside. Across the street he had the massive iron door from

Kehoe's cell, along with the heavy chains and the ring bolt which held the chains to the stone floor. Joe advised that Kehoe was given the choice of the leg or arm chains.

We returned to the barroom and Joe told us that Kehoe was born in Ireland, coming to America with his parents and receiving the spare education usual to the poor of that time. Black Jack had started in the mines as a child, also not unusual for the time and his circumstances. He managed to become a publican, more of a status job then than now. To a publican, politics was a natural adjunct, and soon he was the High Constable of Girardville, a position of power and prestige. He was only 41 when he was hung that early December day in 1878, a victim not only of his own acts-he had bragged about the murder-but of the implacability of Franklin Gowen, who shared the same Irish passion not for justice but for revenge.

As Wayne talked I was studying the Kehoe picture. He was a dark man with piercing and shrewd eyes, a narrow face and a dark mustache and a Prince Imperial goatee. His face evidenced a man of domination, direction and decision. The picture itself still dominated the bar over a hundred years after his death, just as he had dominated the valleys during his short lifetime. I wondered how McParland had been able to fool such a shrewd man.

The small room behind the barroom had seen its share of drama also, not only as the nerve center of the Mollies but because of several meetings with McParland, who had become an officer of the Mollies. I knew that Mrs. Kehoe had accused McParland of being a spy and that Kehoe himself had been suspicious of him. McParland must have been made of strong stuff to do what he did and to do it for almost three years, in the face of such suspicion.

A very brave McParland had come to this very place in the last days of his imposture to demand a hearing on the charges of being a spy. And Kehoe had granted the demand and let him leave. What an interplay of power and courage that must have been.

We discussed the Raven Run killings, of which one of Kehoe's brothers-in-law was convicted, and Wayne told us that Sanger and Uren, the victims, were buried nearby in the Odd Fellows Cemetery, a Protestant benevolent and fraternal organization most popular after the Civil War. We drove there, although only a few blocks away. It was situated on a handsome wooded hill behind which was an even larger hill made of mine tailings. Joe took us directly to the graves, and on inquiry as to why he knew where they were located he told us that he had taken care of the graves as a civic responsibility for several years; another irony in a place of ironies.

Joe Wayne was the right man to ask about Wiggins Patch, for the people murdered there were relatives. Patch in Pennsylvania parlance means a very small settlement, and through the years it had at some point been rechristened Boston Run. The Patch was only four or five miles away and just before one arrived there one saw a still functioning colliery, grey and monstrous, grotesquely mediating between the earth's crust and its rich depths.

Boston Run, formerly Wiggins Patch, turned out to be quite literally a wide place in the road. There are a few houses paralleling the road, holding themselves precariously to the hillsides, with mountains of coal spill and mine tailings behind and above the hills. If there were a dozen houses I would be surprised, all of them were unpainted and many untenanted. It lacked even Arkansas affluence, where one or more inoperable refrigerators on a front yard constituted a conspicuous display of wealth.

Here on December 10th, 1875 a vigilante group, their identities forever concealed behind masks and oilskins, broke into the home of Widow O'Donnell and in the melee which followed, a pregnant daughter and a son were killed. We had seen some copies of newspaper reports which contained drawings of the widow O'Donnell's house and it was still there, just as Joe Wayne had said it was, silent and deserted. It was more than that though; it was derelict and dismal, and it had that look about it which tragedy forever stamps.

A few hours after the murders, a coroner's inquest was held in the living room of the simple three story frame house built against the hill. In the middle of the inquest Kehoe stormed in and directed his sister-in-law not to answer any question as to whether she recognized any of the killers, adding ominously "this business will be settled in another manner."

We stood by the house, uneasily feeling the unsettling emanations. Houses do absorb the happenings within their walls. It was a house of violence and just looking at it caused us both to involuntarily shudder. One of the articles about the house mentioned a bloodstain on the floor which could not be removed. Audrey wanted to go in but the claim about the blood on the floor kept me out. To this day I don't know if I was fearful of not finding it or of finding it.

The narrator of *Valley of Fear* inexplicably omitted any reference to what was called the Wiggins Patch Massacre. It was a curious omission because it showed McParland's bitter ire at the shooting of a woman and his attempt to resign because he anticipated that Mollie counter-violence would now be directed against women and children. A portion of his report to his superiors in Philadelphia stated:

> "I will no longer interfere as I see one is the same as the other and I am not going to be accessory to the murder of women and children.... I am sure the Sleepers will not spare the women and children so long as the Vigilantes have shown the example."[4]

* * *

We left for Raven Run early the next morning under a surly sky which became seething and then poured. It is located in a high valley near the top of the mountains above Shenandoah. It was at Raven Run where on September 1, 1875 Sanger and Uren were shot on the main and only thoroughfare by the Mollies because they represented management, and one of the Widow O'Donnell's boys was found guilty of the murders. It was a pleasant but damp drive, ascending though clean forests which were verdantly, vibrantly green, in fact almost offensively so. There was a small settlement remaining by the name of Raven Run but one of the inhabitants advised that the original townsite had been engulfed years before by the breakers and the mines. Some few of the buildings were moved to the new site, but the murder location was now a hole in the ground.

In *Valley*, the Crow Hill Mine is an obvious substitution for Raven Run Mine, and Dunne and Menzies, the two men there murdered, obviously represented Sanger and Uren.

There was little reason to linger at Raven Run and we drove through the rain to Tamaqua, the last site and the home of Tamaqua Bodymaster Jimmy Kerrigan and nearby Old St. Jerome's Cemetery. Tamaqua was another mining town, indistinguishable from the others which we had seen. The town had started in the narrow valley but had expanded up the abutting hillsides as if it had been squeezed by the valley like a tube of toothpaste. The hillside and hilltop houses were scattered check by jowl in a disorderly array and oddly angled. Van Gelder Street, where my research had told me was the location of the dwarfish Powderkeg Kerrigan's home, was straighter than the other streets and was on the crest of one of the many hills. There were no house numbers in the early 1870's and it was difficult to determine the age of any of the houses because of siding and other triumphs of the subtle arts of the remodeler.

Unlike Jack McMurdo, James McParland found no Elsie Shafter in Tamaqua, or if he did, he did not leave with her, as did Jack. McParland left as he came, alone. Not that he was immune to the more captivating charms of the ladies, for by his own admission he was happy to leave Chicago because of the manipulating marital snares of a Chicago lady, and there were two ladies with Mollie connections whom he "sparked," to use his own phrase. One was more serious than the other, Mary Ann Higgins, Kerrigan's sister-in-law, whom he characterized as vivacious. As he explained in his later court testimony, "It was not for the sake of throwing off suspicion on Kerrigan's part that I made love to his sister-in-law but to throw off any suspicion there might be as to my object in stepping around Tamaqua." McParland was seeking information from Kerrigan as to the killer of a Tamaqua policeman shot while turning down a gas street lamp, but he did have some feeling for her, for he also said in his court testimony:

> "Only once during the whole time did I feel bad, and that was when I looked down and saw Mary Ann sitting there. She was a fine, decent girl and maybe if I'd been the marryin' type, or if we'd met under different circumstance, something would have come of it. As it was, I hate to think of what I did to her pride. She must have thought all I wanted out of her was to use her to trap Kerrigan."

We wanted to see Old St. Jerome's Cemetery for two reasons: the first because it was there that McParland twice maneuvered Kerrigan and where he had his contact hidden behind a tombstone; but neither time did he get any admission out of Powderkeg. The second reason was that it was the cemetery where Joe Wayne advised me his great grandfather, Black Jack Kehoe, was buried so long ago.

This was the proper kind of day to visit a cemetery. The rain had not reached Tamaqua but dark clouds were converging, probably described as dun-colored in the Canon, and an unseasonable raw wind had come up. The air was damp with a penetrating chill and the wind made mournful sounds through the tree limbs. On the ground last year's leaves were being desultorily picked up and swirled around by a fitful wind.

The cemetery was perched on the downward slope of the hill and was small, with houses on three sides. No church was visible and I suspected that it had relocated. This was not an area where large contributions could be expected. The tombstones had every indicia of age, abundant lichen and moss, and the stones, victims alike of time and frost, were sticking out at odd angles like the houses. The cemetery was far from filled, which would have permitted walks by McParland and Kerrigan, and did provide a panoramic view of the valley below. I suspected that this may have been the Miller's Hill mentioned in the Canon but I do not recall if there was the Canonical flagpole.

The Kehoe tombstone was in a desolate corner of the cemetery, as if apologetic that it was there at all. It was difficult to decipher the inscription on it, but this is our joint rendering:

> "Sacred to the memory of
> John Kehoe
> A native of county Wicklow, Ireland
> Died Dec. 18, 1878
> Age 41 years, 5 mo. & 15 days
> May his soul rest in peace. Amen.
> Whilst in this silent grave I sleep
> My soul to God I give to keep."

Below was a notation that Mary died in 1885 at the age of 37.

* * *

Our journey into the Pennsylvania of McParland and the Mollies was about finished. There was only one more stop, and that was tangential, being the reconstruction called Eckley, where a typical mining town and colliery were conveniently assembled. The parts were genuine but the whole was not. You would have seen it if you saw the film *The Mollie Maguires*. The drabness was there but what was a significant omission was the everpresent and pervasive coal dust, which invaded everything, including the miner's lungs.

As we were leaving Schuylkill County Audrey and I talked about the Mollies. It is true that conditions then were bad, and the mine owners less than uncaring, but I had to acknowledge that was the temper of the times. And while one should be congratulated for thinking ahead of one's times, it is not fair to be condemned because one is unable to do so. For their part, the Mollies responded to extreme economic duress with great violence, including assassination by accommodation, and generally to no worthwhile purpose. The killings were vengeful and did not advance labor's cause, but then they were never intended so to do. What the mine owners did lacked the drama of violence and thus tends to merge into nothingness, but if they did not kill by act they did by inaction and lack of help.

It is an odd thing that the desperadoes of yesterday, the James Brothers, Billy the Kid, John Dillinger, and even Pretty Boy Floyd, have, by some populist alchemy, become folk heroes of sorts, fighters against the tyranny of vested interests. This is happening to the Mollies now, and they have been adopted by labor as heroes, but to one who knew them, McParland, they were in his own words indicted as "murderous micks."

We felt more sympathy for the workers after seeing the conditions under which they worked and lived and while violence is unfortunately too often the answer, violence does solve some problems. It was organized labor and not the Mollies' violence which helped the miners, but that is not our problem. We are searching for sites and not social issues.

We were satisfied that we had found what was still there, and since the persona of James McParland is what permeates all, it is not important which side of the fence your prejudices place you in the dispute between the Mollies and management. What is significant is the dangerous journey of James McParland. It deserves to be remembered and respected, for the courage and integrity and determination of this Irishman represents the best hope of the race.

NOTES

1. Donald L. Miller and Richard E. Sharpless, *The Kingdom of Coal: Work, Enterprise, and Ethnic Communities in the Mine Fields* (University of Pennsylvania Press: Philadelphia, PA, 1985, p. 160).
2. For whatever social worth it has, I am convinced of the existence of the sisterhood and its power, despite the changing combinations of its members and occasional internecine disputes over coveted merchandise in short supply, whether material or men, or wearing the same dress. It is an organization without dollar dues (although I am told the dues are onerous) or officers, but the password is the phrase "will you go to the ladies room with me?" and the destination is the club house where the short term plans of the association are discussed and agreed upon, which rather neatly makes explicable the inexplicable amount of time spent there. Now that you have this information it is up to you to do something about it. What that is, I don't know.)
3. Published by Trident Press in New York in 1971.
4. James D. Horan, *The Detective Dynasty That Made History*, cited *supra*.

The Exodus

THE BIBLICAL EXODUS was replicated in the professional life of James McParland, although his years in the wilderness were telescoped from forty years to nearer forty months.

The final paragraph before the Epilogue in the *Valley of Fear* reads: "From Chicago he was chased, after two attempts so near success that it was sure that the third would get him. From Chicago he went under a changed name to California, and it was there that the light went for a time out of his life when Ettie Edwards died."

The Pinkerton records show that McParland — the Doylean Birdie Edwards and John Douglas — did return to Chicago after his Pennsylvania disappearance and as it was not part of the agreement that he would testify against the Mollies, but only to provide information so that they could be charged and convicted, there was no concern for his safety. When however, the prosecution insisted upon his testimony, McParland did not refuse, even though the risk was great, for he was one of those unusual people — a very brave man. As we know, he did testify, and his testimony smashed the Mollies, and secured their convictions and there was not an unreasoned fear that his life was forfeit, or at the very least, at hazard, so a determination was made that he should be secretly spirited from Chicago and placed in a safe house, to remain there until the danger diminished.

That blizzardy afternoon a little over a month before in New York when I met with the Pinkerton personnel director, O'Neill, he mentioned in the course of the discussion that Allan Pinkerton had a country home somewhere near Chicago and that it was there where McParland was hidden. He could not recall the name of the town, but he did remember that some years before the house was going to be razed and one of the town fathers sought, unsuccessfully, Pinkerton's help to save it.

Later, when I called him, he remembered the name of the town, improbably called Onarga. In checking the atlases I did find it, some eighty miles straight south of Chicago, and perilously near Indiana. Now, in another snowstorm, I was travelling my wintery way toward Onarga, There is a horizontality to these plains, a dead level monotony, not unexpected as this was the bottom of a great and ancient glacial lake, of which Lake Michigan is the remaining unevaporated residue, like a minuscule amount of water in a bird bath.

Onarga was a small and very rural community crouching close to the prairie with the tallest structure being two stories in height, as if the result of some unspoken horizontal compact. The Chinese philosopher who insisted that the wise love hills and the virtuous water would have eschewed Onarga — and most of the rest of Illinois.

There was no one in the office of the Onarga *Leader-Review*, which was too bad as newspaper offices are always a providential and prodigious source of local information. But all was not lost for two houses away was a source of even greater information, a beauty parlor. Between the beautician and the customer much data was quickly conveyed. Yes, the Pinkerton place was still there; yes it had suffered through the years, and now it was used as an immigrant workers dormitory for the Bork Nursery, the town's biggest operation; yes, lunch can be obtained at the Tilstra Cafe, but don't ask about the food — the last non-native who inquired in advance about the size of the hamburger was asked to leave.

A telephone call to the Bork Nursery put me in touch with one of the younger Borks who extended permission to photograph the outside of the Pinkerton house but denied permission to enter it. Another call, this one to the local librarian, resulted in a promise to meet me there at 1:30 with what materials she could unearth on the Pinkerton estate.

The first stop was the house, situated a mile or so north of the village. It was surrounded by plantings of the Bork Nursery and was situated about a mile from the road, a drab one story house, squat from a distance and squalid up close. The only redeeming architectural feature was a cupola, and if you had seen this house in passing you would have not given even a first glance, much less the proverbial second. It was a bare, ground- hugging box-like building with no landscaping, no trees, and no bushes. Strips of visqueen, once performing the function of storm windows, fluttered and flapped in the cold wind. It was disappointing not only in its present condition but I wondered how it could ever had been regarded as a country home. The frozen air and my disappointment combined to dictate some of the fastest shots since war photography, and besides, my stomach was empty.

It was lunchtime at the Tilstra Cafe, offering the standard Middlewestern fare of breaded tenderloin or hot roast beef sandwiches. Assiduously following the advice of my local mentor I asked no questions, was not denied a lunch and now it was time to gain brave the cold blasts. I had outrun the snowstorm but I knew it was headed this way and I was anxious to get on to Chicago with as much dispatch as possible, for a major Great Plains snowstorm possesses a majesty and a fury all its own. It drives the wise to shelter and the animals to ground, for it shrieks and sweeps and pounds.

The librarian was there as promised with a massive amount of material piled up on one of the library tables, an impressive performance on such short notice, and I thought of Alan Seegar's lines:

> And I to my pledged word am true
> I shall not fail my rendezvous.

It was a Carnegie library, another thoughtful and generous gift to his adopted country, but built economically as befits a Scottish gift, according to the fewer than half a dozen plans. There was the usual, universal library smell, of deteriorating paper and drying ink, oddly comforting. I stood over the floor register, a reminder of the almost vanished boyhood delights at my parent's and grandparent's home's, now as then a great winter spot to read. The materials were in a series of manilla folders (mistakenly regarded by me as vanilla folders because of the color for altogether too many grade school years) containing brittle and yellowed newspaper clippings, some letters, and those type and photostated extracts from books — a tribute to the tedious Pre-photocopying period.

Two of the newspapers contained stories about James McParland spending two years "hiding out" at the estate. They were not contemporary accounts, which have a verisimilitude of their own as to details, but the sweep of contemporary conclusions should always be suspect, however the accounts were confirmatory of what I had earlier learned at Pinkerton headquarters in New York.

There were pictures of the house, which was much more elaborate than the sad remains, and which I soon learned was not a country retreat but performed the function of a weekend party house, being referred to by the natives a as "Mr. Pinkerton's whoopie house." That phrase conveyed the ring of truth across the years.

The estate, called the Larches because of the 85,000 larch trees which Pinkerton imported from his native Scotland, was 264 acres in size, and while acquired in 1864 the house was not built until 1873. From the drawings and pictures of the house, it was apparent that it originally possessed a veranda extending along all four sides, affording much better lines than the pitiful truncated boxlike structure of today which resembled nothing so much as a Mississippi tenant farmer's house.

I had wondered why the Larches had been built in Onarga, a not very prepossessing site after all, rather than in the area around Dundee where Pinkerton first settled in Illinois and where his cooper shop had been located. Now I had my answer; Onarga was planned and settled by the Illinois Central Railroad, with which both Lincoln and Pinkerton were associated, and which was Pinkerton's number one client. And railroads were intolerant masters. Once Abraham Lincoln was obliged to sue the Illinois Central for his fee, which the court granted him, and the railroad had the temerity to print a little book about it. It is now a Lincoln collectors item, and is one of the things owned by my partner, Angela Simon, who collects the lawyer Lincoln and always concludes her jury arguments with a Lincoln quotation.

The interior of the house was bisected by a central hall, some fifty feet long, containing murals of Scotland and the Civil War. On one side there were four bedrooms and on the other three public rooms. One of the rooms was soundproofed, surely a question-raising matter and certainly not the customary decor, even for a party house. No explanations were offered by the newspapers.

It was now clear from all accounts that the house was never a family retreat but one used for weekend frolics for Pinkerton's guests. According to the papers they arrived from Chicago by rail in private railroad cars of the Illinois Central which were shunted onto a private siding within the confines of the estate. Three cooks were reported to have always been on duty there and the estate contained a race track, a swimming pool and other weekend enticements. Several locals had reported an extensive network of subterranean rooms and chambers, and it seemed from the newspaper accounts that this local gossip, handed down generationally, had its origin in the Snuggery or winehouse, which was partly underground and reached by a tunnel from the house.

Certainly there was an aura of mystery about the villa, an attitude still prevalent among the Onarga natives. (Onargans perhaps?) They still speak of a complete subterranean house of mirror image dimensions below the existing house and a tunnel from the railroad spur some distance away. Undoubtedly these persisting village tales have their genesis in the half-underground drinking room, and doubtlessly the guards which Pinkerton had around the perimeter of the estate would add further fuel to the fire of gossip about the weekend activities and give credence to the festivity rumors. I had begun to suspect that the guards may have been there for McParland's protection during his surreptitious stay there, and certainly it was at least partly so, but I also recalled the immobile uniformed guard at the entrance to the Pinkerton corporate headquarters. Since protection was one of the Pinkerton products it was a shrewd self-endorsement.

Certainly the Larches was the ideal place for McParland to have remained hidden for the two years that tradition suggests, and accordingly the villa, or whoopie house, whichever is the more appropriate designation, has a claim to inclusion in the greater Holmesian Canon for its *bona fides* are clear.

That night in Chicago, as I looked out of my room in the Raphael Hotel and into the mighty maw of horizontal snow seemingly continuously headed for the nearby lake, I thought about McParland, who despite a labor bias against him still, had to be recognized as a man of courage and consequence, and one who followed his beliefs through privation and even peril. And it occurred to me that this was the proper place to consider these matters, for it was here in Chicago where the saga commenced, and where James McParland entered the Canon. It turned out to be a giant step into the Pinkerton pantheon and from there into literary immortality.

The Great-Hearted Soldier

ONE OF THE CHARACTERS in many melodramas, that nineteenth century descendant of the miracle plays of the Middle Ages, was the Great-Hearted Soldier.

He appears in the Canon, albeit briefly, but significantly, for it was his action which provided the initial flesh to the character of Doctor John H. Watson, and it is very appropriate to conclude with him as the final real person in the Canon.

ALEXANDER FRANCIS PRESTON

It was an episode occurring in the Second Afghan War which triggered a possibility in the mind of a young and largely unsuccessful medical practitioner in the wilds of Southsea, on the south coast of England. He had followed that war; wars interested him, and I have always been a bit surprised that Doyle did not himself become a military surgeon.

Our Great-Hearted Soldier was Surgeon-Major Alexander Francis Preston of the Army Medical Department, who while treating an injured soldier in the lost battle of Maiwand, was himself grievously wounded. Those in that battle were directed to prepare a narrative report, and a copy of Preston's own account was obtained by me from the Ministry of Defence Library at the Old War Office Building in Whitehall. That account follows, which, while extensive, is quoted in its entirety because of its interest.

From Surgeon-Major A.F. Preston, Army Medical Department, to the Adjutant General, Poona — (No. 26, dated Clarinda Park, West, Kingstown, the 14 December 1880).

In compliance with the instructions contained in your letter No. 2886-A, dated the 16th November, 1880, I have the honor to report, for the information of His Excellency the Commander in Chief in India, the circumstances connected with the actions at Maiwand and the subsequent retreat to Kandahar which came under my personal observation.

I must, however, premise by saying that as I was wounded rather early in the day (about 1 o'clock p.m.) and removed from the scene of action, I am unable to record from personal observation, anything that occurred between that hour and about 3 o'clock p.m., when the rout commenced.

On the morning of the 27th July, Brigadier-General Burrow's brigade, to which I, as medical officer in charge of the 66th Regiment, belonged, marched at an early hour from Khushki-i-Nakhud, where we had been encamped for some days previously. We were informed that the fort at Maiwand had been occupied by some *ghazis*, whom it was considered necessary to dislodge.

After we have proceeded about eight miles on our way towards Maiwand, some cavalry were seen about two miles off to our left front. We changed our direction and made towards them. On our advancing, they retired. We continued in their direction, and after we had crossed a deep *nallah* and arrived at the ground they had just left, we found ourselves confronted by an army, which, notwithstanding the mirage and the distance intervening between us and them (which was considerable), we could easily make out a very large one.

We were at once placed in the following formation — the 66th on the right, the 30th Bombay Native Infantry in the center, and the 1st Bombay Native Infantry on the left, with guns at intervals.

The ground on which we took up our positions was a perfectly bare *maidan*, without a particle of cover or protection of any kind, and lower than that occupied by the enemy, which was slightly elevated and sloped gradually towards the hills in their rear. Even for my hospital establishment there was absolutely no cover. It was exposed all through to the fire of the enemy.

No time was lost on our side in attacking, the horse artillery commencing the action with their guns at about 10 o'clock a.m., at 2000 yards.

The enemy did not reply for some time but when they did, their fire was well directed, and both shells and cannon balls fell amongst us in great numbers.

Shortly after the action had commenced, the enemy, who had been working their way down nearer to us, began pouring out cavalry in great numbers from their flanks, with the evident intention of closing in on us and surrounding us.

This movement on their part from their left flank was checked by the volley firing of the 66th Regiment (who had up to this period been passive) at about 1100 yards. The regiment after this was ordered to lie down. Shortly afterwards, whilst attending to a wounded man of the 66th Regiment, I was myself dangerously wounded and carried off the field. I am therefore unable, from personal observation, to state what took place subsequently, until the rout commenced at about 3 o'clock p.m.

After my wounds had been attended to, I was lying quietly in my *duli*, imagining that all was going on well as regarded the day, the idea of our losing it never entering my thoughts, when all of a sudden my *duli*-bearers took up the *duli* and commencing running off with me as fast they could go, shouting, as they ran along, that the *ghazis* were on us. I raised the curtain of the *duli* and looked out, and, to my great surprise, saw a regular stampede, man and animals making off as hard as they could; all in utter confusion; no order of any kind; but everybody evidently bent on doing the utmost to save his own life and get out of the way of danger as fast and as best he could. With this object all the loads had been thrown off from the baggage animals, which were at once appropriated for riding purposes. The ground all about was, in consequence, covered with camp equipage, boxes of ammunition and treasure, mess stores, wines, &c.

My *duli*-bearers had not carried me far before they deserted me to a man, and after two other modes of conveyance in which

I had been placed that afternoon had failed, I was finally taken up by a horse artillery wagon. All this time the stampede had been going on, and men (white and black) horses, camels, bullocks, &c., passed me in endless confusion.

After I had been placed on the wagon, it was impossible for me to see much of what was going on, as I was in a recumbent position and surrounded by men, wounded and otherwise, who were riding on the wagon along with me.

Travelling in this way all night through the desert, we arrived at the village of Ashu-Khan next morning at about 4 o'clock, and here we got water for first time since the previous morning. En route we passed several men, European and Native, who had lain down in the desert, overcome by exhaustion and want of water.

At Ashu-Khan the horses were taken out of the wagon to be watered, and when brought back were so utterly exhausted, that, notwithstanding every effort on the part of the drivers, they could not be got to move.

I lay helpless on the wagon for, I should say, a couple of hours, expecting every moment that some of our party would be shot as the villagers here, as they did all along the road, kept continually firing at us. However, as a few stragglers of the 66th came up, I asked them to stay with me and to use their rifles in return. In this way the villagers were kept off.

After some time a camel with a pair of *kajawas* came up. Apothecary Cordeiro, of the Subordinate Medical Department (Bombay) who had been walking all night, came up about the same time. He stopped the camel and had me put into one of the *kajawas*, and, regardless of his own safety, remained by me for a long time and did everything in his power to assist me.

I had not proceeded far in the *kajawa* before the cords binding it together commenced giving way, and, to save me from falling, the camel had to be made to lie down quickly.

Whilst going along in the *kajawa*, I was passed by Brigadier-General Burrows and Nutall; and, whilst lying helpless on the ground in the broken *kajawa*, I was passed by a large party of Sind Horse under the command of Colonel Malcolmson.

After I had been lying on the ground for some time, Captain Slade, Royal Horse Artillery, came up with one of the smooth-bore guns, and seeing me and the situation I was in, at once determined on endeavoring to save my life and not leave me in my inevitable fate. His horses were so utterly beaten, that they would not have been equal to my additional weight; so, in order to save my life, he abandoned the gun and have me put upon the limber. Even then it was only by his splendid tact and management, his presence of mind and great coolness in danger (for the inhabitants kept firing at us all along), that he succeeded in getting the horses to move at all. He carried me as far as Kokeran on the limber. I was there transferred to a *dandi* which had accompanied C-2nd Royal Artillery, under the late Brigadier-General Brooke, and this brought me into Kandahar, which I reached about 4 o'clock on the afternoon of the 28th.

I fear that it will be thought that a very large portion of this letter is taken up with irrelevant matter which refers only to myself; but in endeavoring to describe the little that came under my personal observation during the retreat on Kandahar, I found it impossible to avoid this.

War brings out the best and worst in people, (and defeat imposes even greater demands) its pressures transforming bravery into heroism and fear into cowardice. Both were apparent in Preston's candid report, with more credit to the lower ratings than to the higher. But for Sherlockians, there is some very significant stuff here: the absence of any gallant young Murray and the presence of more than one wound to Preston.

Preston's own account of the battle of Maiwand modestly omitted his courageous conduct. According to the records of the Royal Army Medical Corps, at "…the battle of Maiwand in which he was severely wounded whilst attending a disabled man in the front line of fire."

There is a note reminiscent of our Doctor Watson in Preston's life. "He retired on half pay on 16 October 1881 and returned to full pay on 4 May 1882 as a Brigade Surgeon…"

Preston went on to a long and distinguished career in military medicine, and led a pleasant and full life. He died in

1907 and his obituary in the *British Medical Journal* follows:

> Many readers will have seen with great regret the announcement of the death of Surgeon General Alexander Francis Preston, who was well known both at Montreux and on the Riviera. He was only in his 65th year, but he had seen much service. He was a son of the late Rev. D.W. Preston, Rector of Killinkere and Rural Dean, his mother being a daughter of General Armstrong, R.A. His grandfather was judge of appeal and his grandmother was daughter and co-heiress of the 5th Baron Carbery. Having graduated B.A. and M.B. at Trinity College, Dublin, he entered the Army Medical Service in 1863. He served in India, Afghanistan and China; was in medical charge of the 66th Regiment in Afghanistan in 1880, and was severely wounded in two places at Maiwand. He was all through the siege of Kandahar, being mentioned in dispatches, and promoted to Lieutenant-Colonel. His commissions were thus dated: Assistant-Surgeon, September 30, 1863; Surgeon, March 1, 1873; Surgeon-Major, April 28, 1876; Brigade-Surgeon, November 30, 1886; Surgeon-Colonel, March 28, 1892; Surgeon-General, July 6, 1896. He retired from the service May 23, 1902. In 1901 he was appointed Honorary Physician to Queen Victoria, the appointment being confirmed by King Edward.... He held a Distinguished Service Pension of 100 pounds a year. His great abilities were hidden by his geniality. He was a zealous whist and bridge player, and fond of golf, travel, and sport, being well known at Ranelagh and the Royal Irish Yacht Club.

The Sherlockian will not have missed the reference again to his being wounded in two places at Maiwand. While it confirms the historicity of Watson's wounds, it attests to Watson's failure to explain that there were two.

Preston spent his last years in London, living at 53, Redcliffe Gardens, in Kensington, and dying there. A picture of that house appears in my book, *The Worth of the Game*, as well as a picture of Preston as a young man.

There is one final item remaining about Alexander F. Preston, and it is one of those oddities which abound in research about the Canon. His mother's family had held the Armstrong barony, but their name had not always been Armstrong. Some years before, in default of issue, a great-nephew had assumed the name of Armstrong by license, so as to inherit the title and the estate. His name was — Watson. His father was the master of Adderstone Hall in Northumbria, and his name was — John Watson.

There is little doubt that Doyle had read the reports of the rout at Maiwand. It would have been difficult to have missed them, as the many daily London papers were replete with stories of the disaster. Tragedies still sell newspapers and air time. Doyle added the bit about young Murray and retold the rest of the Preston narrative. Preston's adventure became Watson's adventure, and Watson became Preston, just as Preston became Watson. Thus was one genuine Scot substituted for one fictitious one, and a literary legend was born which has never died.

NOTES

1. Letter to the author from J.O. Campbell dated 13 February 1984, on behalf of the Curator and Secretary of the R.A.M.C. Historical Museum at Aldershot.
2. *Ibid*
3. I have always wondered if Preston was ever aware of his role in the Canon. I hired two researchers to locate his papers and letters, which apparently ended up with the Nixon family, but neither the researchers nor I could ever obtain a response. If you wish to pursue the subject of Preston any further, you should read two articles which my friend Fred Mende of Charlotte, North Carolina, authored in the *Baker Street Journal*. Fred, proceeding as far as he wished in the matter, and in the gentlemanly spirit of the ideal Sherlockian, turned over to me the documents which he had obtained on Preston, including Preston's picture.

The Connecticut Connection

THERE HAVE BEEN MANY portrayers of Sherlock Holmes, but in this country and abroad there have been only three who have swept the public off its feet and kept it in abject but delightful bondage until the retirement of each from the Sherlockian stage.

Strictly speaking, it is arguable that none of the portrayers are real people within the Canon, but because they each *became* Holmes for a time, they were in a very real sense an integral part of the Canon. But if you disagree, exercise your franchise now by skipping to Chapter 23.

The first expositor was William Gillette.[1]

WILLIAM GILLETTE

Autumn is good for Connecticut. It burnishes the landscape clean and bright. Today was November 23rd, a Saturday, and I was driving leisurely and easterly on Interstate 95 from New Haven in what met every unfortunate test of being a rented car, on my way to Haddam on the Connecticut River. It was football weather, cold and clear and crisp; indeed this was a football weekend, with Harvard playing Yale at the Yale bowl. My pleasure however was quite different; no weekend half-retreats to collegiate days nor whole retreats to the gladiatorial violence of Neronian Rome. (Daddy, how much longer do we have to wait until the Christians come on?) For me this was far more personal; no quest for an unidentified site this time, but a sentimental return to a place I had never been.

My destination was William Gillette's castle, by any technical standard not a legitimate site, yet in a way it was a strictly Sherlockian adventure as he was for many people the very personification of Holmes. For the Pre-Rathbone generations he was Holmes, essential, quintessential and incarnate. His home, which was so much of himself, as any genuine home should be, properly belongs in any listing of Holmesian sites.

Driving that bright morning, I thought a good deal about Gillette. He was born in 1853, the sensitive son of patrician parents who gave him an idyllic childhood in the Hartford, Connecticut area, and who in their wisdom permitted him to skip college and become an actor, and that at a time when it was more than a notorious craft. Entertainer was a fluid term - Nathaniel Hawthorne called such terms portmanteau words - and included the activities of many ladies who performed more frequently off stage than on. Indeed, it is no accident that even today the reference is to the legitimate theater.

He fell deeply in love with Helen Nickles of Detroit, and they were married in 1882, but they did not live happily ever after. Their marriage was idyllic but she died at age 28 in 1888 of a not uncommon killer then, a ruptured appendix. Gillette's health had never been particularly robust and he had suffered from digestive and intestinal problems which were aggravated by overwork and anxiety. After his wife's death he went into what was termed in the language of the time as a decline. He was ill and became a virtual recluse for five years. In 1892 he withdrew to mountainous Tryon, North Carolina, where he had a two room cabin built a mile from the nearest town.

Later he had worked his way back into the theater. He called it his "upward start." Charles Frohman, then a young theater entrepreneur, became his friend and colleague, producing plays written by Gillette.

No taint of immorality ever attached itself to Gillette, and after the early death of his young wife he remained faithful to her memory. He was in many ways a sad, driven man, and he sought to exorcise or at least mitigate that sadness by deepening his acting craft and extending himself collaterally as a playwright. But the loneliness seeped out in his nocturnal walks which ended in exhausted sleep, whether on a bench or on the ground.

His productions, written, acted and directed by him, bore distinctively nineteenth century titles: *The Professor, The Private Secretary, Held by the Enemy, Too Much Johnson,* and *Secret Service,* the last being his most successful play before his Holmes productions. He appeared on stage both here and in England, becoming a millionaire in the process and raising the theater to a high level of professionalism at the same time he was reaching large audiences. It is known that Doyle saw him act in London at the Adelphi Theatre in *Secret Service* but it is not definitively known if he ever saw him appear as Sherlock Holmes.

In 1898 Frohman obtained Doyle's consent for Gillette to transform the Holmes stories into a stage vehicle. Gillette wrote it a few weeks, but it was burned in a San Francisco hotel fire but Gillette quickly wrote it again. Doyle gave him virtually unlimited latitude in constructing the plot, even to the point of permitting Gillette to introduce a love interest for the misogynistic Holmes.

Audrey and I had been at the Hindhead Railway Station where Doyle and Gillette first met in May of 1899 and where Doyle is quoted as almost involuntarily saying "Holmes" and Gillette "Watson." It is a delightful story and therefor one hopes it is true, rivaling as it does the even less laconic Stanley-Livingstone meeting, but it is probably apocryphal as Doyle had seen Gillette act and knew his lineaments. And in any event Doyle originally envisioned a much uglier Holmes with deep-set, close-set eyes and Gillette was strikingly handsome, but then perhaps Doyle's view of Holmes had been influenced by the Paget drawings.

The play *Sherlock Holmes* was a hit from the beginning and easily became Gillette's most celebrated stage vehicle. It opened in Buffalo at the Star Theater in the fall of 1899, and premiered at the Garrick in New York in November. Gillette appeared in the role some 1300 times, with total receipts being over a million and a half dollars.

The American company opened in London at the Lyceum Theater — you will recall its significance in the Canon — in September 1901, appearing before King Edward VII, with the King coming afterward to his dressing room. The King had visited many dressing rooms but not often to see male actors. Doyle also was kind to the company, entertaining it at his country home, Undershaw, on Christmas Day of 1901.

Holmes come to dominate Gillette as he had Doyle. Gillette played Holmes up until a few years before his death in 1937, including some radio performances and several farewell tours as Holmes. He was Sherlock Holmes to those who grew up in the 30 years from 1899 to 1929, and indeed his physical imprint on Holmes was definitive for some years beyond his death; at least until 1939 when Basil Rathbone confidently assumed the Sherlockian mantle. It was Rathbone, no mean scholar in his own right, and a man eloquent in his own words, who once quoted a materialized Watson as telling him in Central Park, "goodbye my friend, . . . never regret anything you have attempted with sincere affection. Nothing is lost that is born of the heart."

Audrey enjoys *Country Life* and it does give insights into the British character. The only problem, aside from its exorbitant cost, is that it arrives each week, and she is somewhere back in 1937 in her catch-up reading.

Occasionally, however, she shares a tidbit with me, and one recently was an article with some Sherlockian significance, entitled, T*he Smoking Detective*, which actually was a reprint of an article contemporary with the Gillette production of Holmes. The reporter claimed the distinction of suggesting a smoking detective, an idea which Gillette embraced, whether at his own instance or not. Holmes of course did smoke, using all the varietals, but seeking greater ease in stage-speaking, Gillette introduced the calabash pipe. As a former chain pipe smoker I can assure that the calabash was never a good smoke, and I smoked several of them, because the calabash is a gourd. Its prominence occurred in the Boer War as field expedients for the Tommies. The superstition about three on a match also had its genesis then, for by the time the third man had drawn his light Brother Boer had time to draw his bead.

The salt-smell of the Sound caused me to recollect that Gillette had been quite a yachtsman, with a substantial yacht incongruously named the Aunt Polly. In fact, he was on that vessel cruising on the Connecticut River in 1912 when he first saw the crag named the Seventh Sister, which so captured his fancy that he built his crypto-castle on its imposing eminence.

I recalled that he had spent more than a million Pre-WWI dollars on the construction of his dream house, and in the money of our time it would have cost ten or twelve times as much now. It became at once his great dream and his most special place. He was more than the driving force of the project; he drew the plans, supervised the construction and even designed a trolley arrangement for moving materials vertically from the riverbank to the work site on the top of the Seventh Sister. And as the work advanced, what had started in his mind as a rustic lodge become a castle.

I had arrived at the west bank of the river, not mighty like the Mississippi nor lordly like the Hudson, but a respectably-sized river and one once so appealing to Henry Thoreau that he travelled on it and wrote a celebrated book about his voyage. For me it was a short ride northerly paralleling the river and then across the bridge to the east.

I broke my pilgrimage at the Gelston House, an 1854 Italianate hotel smartly situated above the site of the East

Haddam Ferry Slip, enjoying there a pleasant Shore Lunch, made memorable by one of my favorite desserts, Indian Pudding, well worthy of capitalization.

After lunch I proceeded to gingerly trek upward in wide circles past considerable woods and an occasional hardscrabble farmstead. The entire ambiance was one of solicitous rurality rather than unsolicitous urbanity. It reminded me of the home bluffs along the northern Mississippi and could sense how much pleasure the theatrical Gillette would have obtained in the approach to his castle. The drive upland to the castle was theatrical in every sense of the word. I knew why Gillette so loved this place and I expected higher drama at the Castle, for wise actors carefully built to an ordered climax.

The State of Connecticut owns and operates the castle as a state park, and there was not much question that the state regarded Gillette's role as being the great expositor of Mr. Holmes, for at the entrance to the walk up to the castle, a sign portrayed Gillette's profile and written above it was the legend, Sherlock Holmes, and below the profile were Gillette's name and birth and death dates. Significantly, no birth or death dates were attributed to Holmes. I liked the place already.

I moved forward with new confidence, and walking up the short footpath through the woods, I had my first glimpse of the castle. It was a towering structure, but one seemingly melting, as if it were a gigantic ice cream castle on a summer day. No line was clear nor clean nor even distinct. It looked much like Gaudi's agonized architecture in Barcelona. The problem was the stone and its placement, which did suggest that the stone itself was dripping. If he were seeking to replicate a Rhine castle he had failed and somehow it had remained a hunting lodge built by an Arkansas developer. But those of us who are over 200 pounds must intellectually insist that it is what is inside that counts.

I hurried inside the *porte-cochere* and then up the inside stone steps, which to my chagrin I later learned were seventeen in number. Of course. But then I have always claimed that observing is one thing; counting is quite another. So now you have my confession: I am only half-Holmesian, a semi-Sherlockian at best, for they who do not count can enter not the kingdom.

A left turn brings you into the large stone-walled living hall, majestically some 19 feet tall, 30 feet wide, and 50 feet long. It was Hitlerian in dimension and reminded me of the large hall at Berchtesgaden, but then both men were consummate actors.

For the Sherlockian the greatest interest in the room was by the door and it was a bust of Gillette in the guise of Holmes, a handsome thing done in bronze by a sculptor named Anthony Bonadies. Dominating the hall was a massive stone fireplace which is not surprising as in Gillette's other and earlier retreats there were always fireplaces, not excluding his yacht. On the interior wall opposite the fireplace was an open stairway suitable for a grand entrance, connecting to an upstairs hallway which was open to the living hall except for a balustrade. On the river side of the house, opposite to the side from which we entered, and near the corner, was the conservatory, still containing plants and a pool, the latter once the watery refuge of Lena and Mike, a frog couple of Gillette's close acquaintance.

From the conservatory one doubles back into the body of the house and enters the dining room, an unusually small room, more like a breakfast room. I learned that he did not entertain very much at dinner and so size was a function of purpose. Gillette was essentially and pleasantly reclusive, and while gregarious when with people, he preferred privacy. After all, if one is able to live with frogs then why put up with people? On the whole, it may have been not an entirely unwise choice.

The dining table was fixed to a rolling floor track so that instead of moving up to the table it moved up to you. There appeared to be only places for two on the padded bench built against the wall, and like another reclusive New Englander who also liked the same river, perhaps two places were sufficient for companionship and three for society. Opposite was a wooden cabinet which by the manipulation of a secret device would open, revealing a well-stacked bar. I wondered if he was worried about his servants or his frogs?

Beyond the dining room was a small interior chamber and beyond that was a study which opened out to the easterly side of the house. It was a substantial room, and significantly larger than all but the living hall. The study was obviously a working room dominated by an antique desk which was brought from his family home near Hartford. The desk chair was also on floor rails and there was a secret door communicating with the living hall. Outside one could see the woods at the entrance to the castle and I was sure that he wanted a comfortable but disciplined view here, just as he wished a soaring panoramic view from the living hall. His life was obviously his work and he was not a social creature, although surprisingly, he was an easy man with whom to talk. Although he played a public role he lived a very private life, which is not a bad social compromise. While the *bon vivant* actor created the living hall, and the recluse the dining room, it was the writer who conceived the study.

Upstairs is the recreation of the Baker Street sitting room, appropriate and interesting, but surprisingly it was his bedroom which was for me the highlight of the floor. No, you are quite wrong, for I am too old to even remember to reminisce about bedrooms. I fall asleep in them almost instantly. It was the minuscule size of the bedroom and the very spartan simplicity which was astounding. It was a veritable monk's cell. There was a very narrow iron bed, not unlike the old hospital cots—it was an anchorite's bed, which underlined the fact that he was not the usual actor, for they require double beds. There was a simple dressing table, built-in and wooden, evocative of an actor's make-up table and a simple chair rounded out the furniture. But none of these things dominated the room; that was left to an old and frayed dressing gown hanging on the wall the one Gillette used when playing the Great Detective. There was a further oddity here, another trace of the actor, which consisted of two mirrors, one on the balcony outside and the second on his dressing table, both ingeniously placed so as to permit him to watch his guests in the living hall, and presumably to allow him to descend at the most propitious and appropriate time.

On the whole, the inside of the castle was like the outside, with everything a trifle off, like a wine starting to go bad. It was the work of a boy-architect and boy-designer for an adult who was periodically reclusive. The boy devised the gadgetry, including the wooden light switches, but the actor presided. The problem was that each part of Gillette was present here and they gave off different architectonic signals. For me, the boy prevailed; the idea of a castle itself, the secret door, the complex locks, the pervasive gadgetry, the miniature railroad and train, and yes, perhaps even the interest in Sherlock Holmes. And for those of you who may scoff at this suggestion, remember Doyle's own miniature railroad at Hindhead and his own reference to the half-boy and half-man entity for whom he wrote. It is not given to every child to fulfill childhood dreams, and there is no sweeter pleasure. For me, that was the statement of the castle.

I had a reservation at the Griswold Inn at nearby Essex, a hostelry with a tad over 200 years of catering to the travelling public. I looked forward to a couple of quiet before-dinner drinks in the comfortable bar with its handhewn oak ceiling beams and then a leisurely dinner, thus being afforded a double opportunity to ruminate about today's activities in pleasant surroundings. It was not to be.

It was the weekend of the Harvard-Yale football game and doubtlessly in that long catalogue of my mistakes and misjudgments the failure to avoid this weekend will loom large. Vast Harvard contingents had rendezvoused here midmorning and then left for the game at New Haven in an array of buses, returning to the Griswold for continuing drinks, frivolity, perhaps dinner, and early to bed, that is, early the next morning. This was the halfway house from their annual euphoric Bacchanalia in Babylon to their usual New England rigidity, taciturnity and stolidity. It was clearly the last night out and the ship of spirits was docking early the next morning.

Now to me, upright drinking is the grossest of discourtesies to a dry martini, or to any other serious libation for that matter, and it was shoulder-to-shoulder in the bar. I remembered the dean of my old college referring in the freshman convocation to the alumni walking arm in arm on their return to the campus, seeking to recapture something which was lost here forever. I learned from him many years later that it turned out to be the collegiate spirit, and that spirit was never lost by my fellows at the Griswold Inn. I wended my way to bed a bit earlier, selfishly saddened that Harvard had fought fiercely, for failure is more subdued, and while waiting for sleep to finally overcome the last echoes of college mirth winding its way two stories upward from the bar, I could imagine such frivolity in the great hall of the Gillette Castle. I could almost visualize Gillette upstairs, enjoying his solitude above the multitude below, and delighting in delaying the entrance of the public Gillette. I could see him finally, at the *moment d'etre* majestically descending his staircase in even-cadenced liquid motion, like the Duchamps figure in the 1913 Armory show. Holmes himself would have envied the drama of that entrance.

Clearly there was a good deal of Holmes in Gillette and likewise of Gillette in Holmes, for after all it was Gillette who gave Holmes his first three dimensional form, fixing the fictive figure for forty years, which was no mean achievement. Gillette Castle is a must for the serious Sherlockian, and only Michael Harrison, that master of the long drink, ever criticized it to me, and that was because at the Holmesian gatherings there the State of Connecticut interdicts *spiritus frumentus*. One word of caution however, avoid the weekend of the Harvard-Yale game.

NOTES

1. What follows in this chapter was substantially first written in a book of mine entitled *To Play The Game*, published in 1991 by the Gasogene Press. I do not believe in writing something for the sake of writing it, and when I am satisfied that what was once written by me is the best effort which I can muster, I present it a second time, not as a stale leftover, but as my best culinary offering. I do not believe I can do better today than yesterday in my analysis of Gillette the Sherlockian actor, and while the chapter was written about places rather than people, because Gillette's castle was so much a part of him, the analysis is most apposite. It is presented without apology, except that in the years since I have been unable to develop any additional insights in the subject. Poverty in imaginatative insights is a sufficient apologia in itself.

The Literate Portrayer

BASIL RATHBONE was indisputably the second great portrayer, despite the pitiful films to which Holmes had descended. Many were political themes made to buttress the war effort — itself a World War II war-speak phrase — and others were to take peoples' minds off the war momentarily. In my view, the only two films about Holmes which were exceptional were *The Hound of the Baskervilles* and *The Scarlet Claw*. The rest could slip mercilessly into the dark and murky Sherlockian seas, except for Rathbone's portrayal as Holmes, who himself felt that he had early developed the Holmes character and the rest was — not silence — unfortunately. As for his good friend, Willy Bruce, his characterization of Watson was a tour de force of English bumbling, blundering and mumbling. It has put poor Watson as the epitome of *boobus Britannicus*, just as his equivalent, S.S. Van Dine in the Philo Vance stories, epitomizes *boobus Americanus*.

Because Rathbone was a literate person and a fine writer, I am tempted to end this chapter with the injunction to read his autobiography, *In and Out of Character*.[1] Just as a fine-wrought book is a noble thing, when it is a memoir by someone who knows himself, it becomes monumental. This is such a book. I have but one criticism of it, and that his that while he mentions his daughter by his second marriage by name many times, his son by his first marriage merits only one sparse mention and then not even by name. It is a fault far more grievous than mere lit-

BASIL RATHBONE AND NIGEL BRUCE

erary error, and raises some fundamental questions about Rathbone, none of which can be answered on the basis of present data.

There is another significant tell in his book, and that is the powerful influence which his involvement in trench warfare in World War I had upon him — not that battle does not mould forever any man who has had organized death dealt by or toward him. The first chapter in Rathbone's book was this experience, and it appears before his birth and early years.

Rathbone was born on June 13, 1892 in South Africa where his father was an English mining engineer during the troubles between the English and the Boers, but because of those very problems he was brought back to England early on, receiving his education there. He was christened Philip St. John Basil Rathbone, which discloses much.

His family were significant members of the upper middle class in the Liverpool area, and one American relative, Major Rathbone. was with Lincoln at Ford's Theater that tragic night and was stabbed by Booth.

Basil graduated near the bottom of his class at Repton , one of the English public schools, and at his family's behest he agreed to defer his acting plans for a year and work as a junior clerk in the London, Liverpool and Globe

Insurance Company, in which his family had an interest.

His abiding interest in the theater unabated, his kinsman, Sir Frank Benson, took him into his Shakespearean repertory company, playing juvenile leads. A Gemini, like so many other successful players, he found the theater to be the be-all and end-all for him. After the war he played increasingly important roles, not only in Shakespeare but in plays by other authors, but it was in *Peter Ibbetson* at the Savoy Theatre which made him an immediate success. In 1921 he came to America and stayed at the Algonquin, where he became a fast friend of Frank Case, the owner.

In 1926 he married Ouida Bergere, a successful script writer for Paramount Pictures, and the marriage endured until his death. It was a love match for each, and one which he characterized as being a chemical reaction. Love at first sight was an appropriate description for a Hollywood actor. He appeared in many films in this country: *Dawn Patrol, Captain Blood, Robin Hood, Mark of Czar, Last Days of Pompeii*, and *Anna Karenina*. He was also active in the theater, playing leads in *The Barrette of Wimpole Street* and *Romeo and Juliet* opposite Katherine Cornell, and in *JB The Heiress* and *Judas*, among other productions.

His interests were several and deep. They always remained: his wife, his daughter, the theater, music and dogs.

His fame rests upon the frame of Sherlock Holmes, a role which ended up encompassing him as it had Doyle, and accomplishing the same result — each became a hater of Holmes. Almost every portrayer of Holmes has complained of the Holmes persona and the effect upon his career. There is a pattern in this and perhaps someday a savant will address and solve this final Holmesian mystery.

There were many Holmes films, commencing with the one which was easily the best, *The Hound*. For me the only one thereafter which was worth watching was *The Scarlet Claw*, but that is purely a personal view.

Nigel Bruce, his Watson, played the *fidus achates* in such a manner as has stereotyped Watson. Bruce himself was a personal friend of Rathbone, and they are their wives formed a social foursome. Bruce had a Rabelaisian wit which he successfully con-cealed in his Watson personation.

Rathbone played Holmes, according to his own count, in sixteen pictures and some two hundred radio broadcasts, all of which he regarded as being of "exceptionally high quality."[2] Yet the response of reviewers and the public was one of general ridicule of him and his Holmes. As he reported:

> I do not remember a single instance from 1939 to 1962 where an interviewer from some newspaper or magazine, or a member of an audience, or a friend has not smiled somewhat indulgently when the subject of my association with Mr. Sherlock Holmes has arisen. In the upper echelon of my very considerable following as Mr. Holmes, there has always been a somewhat patronizing, if polite, recognition my modest achievement. In the lower echelon I have experienced nothing but embarrassment in the familiar streetcorner greeting of recognition, which is invariably followed by horrendous imitations of my speech, loud laughter, and ridiculing quotes of famous lines such as 'Quick Watson, the needle' or 'Elementary, my dear Watson,' followed by more laughter at my obvious discomfiture.[3]

Rathbone concluded that the timing was bad for Holmes and when he played Holmes it was "too late for a serious presentation."[4] He also believed the stories were dated. Yet, gentleman that Rathbone was, he granted Holmes more than grudging admiration:

> One was jealous of Holmes of course. Yes, of course, that was it. One was jealous. Jealous of his mastery of all things, both material and mystical…he was sort of a god in his own way, seated on some Anglo-Saxon Olympus of his own design and making! Yes, there was no question about it, he had given me an acute inferiority complex![5]

It is not known what was the effect on his psyche of the monumental failure of his wife's play about Holmes, drawn from five of the stories, which bombed on Broadway in 1953, closing after three performances. He did later observe that it was outdated, and wholly ignored by the television generation. We do know that it was his final Holmes venture, and never afterward did he appear as that detective.

He died on July 21, 1967, still unhappily typed as Holmes, the nemesis who destroyed his career. Yet it was Rathbone, something of a mystic, who claimed to foretell what was going to happen to him, wrote of an experience when he met Watson in a Central Park reverie. Watson, according to Rathbone, left him, observing "Goodbye my friend, I am glad to have had this opportunity to talk with you. You must not regret anything you have attempted with a sincere affection. Nothing is lost that is born of the heart."[6]

NOTES

1. Rathbone, Basil, *In and Out of Character*,Doubleday & Company, Garden City, 1962.
2. *Ibid.*, p. 179.
3. *Ibid,*, p. 178.
4. *Ibid.*, p. 179.
5. *Ibid.*, p. 182.
6. *Ibid.*, p. 217.

The Moonlight Portrayer

THE THIRD PORTRAYER of Mr. Holmes was Jeremy Brett. Brett brought Holmes to virtually the start of the twenty-first century, just as William Gillette introduced Holmes to the public near the end of the nineteenth century, and as Basil Rathbone brought the theater imposture into films just before the middle of the twentieth century.

I suspect that it was Brett who came the closest to the real Holmes. He certainly dug the deepest and his performance, even in the later episodes, was truer to the character than Rathbone and probably Gillette. To the latter two performers, Holmes was a thinking machine and they played him as such, controlled and wholly cerebral. In truth and in fact, Holmes had a deeply troubled persona and his cerebral efforts were to control and thus compensate for his self-troubling flaws. Perhaps because Brett too had disabling emotional problems, the resemblance was fortuitous.

JEREMY BRETT

He was born Peter Jeremy William Huggins in 1933, the fourth son in an upper class English family. His parents were Quakers, although, inconsistently, his father was a field-grade officer in the English military during both World Wars. His mother was from the famous chocolate family of Cadbury, well known for their Quaker-inspired benevolences. Jeremy grew up in idyllic circumstances at Berkswell Grange, a seventeenth-century mansion set in the countryside near Manchester. He was educated at Eton, the favored school of the upper classes, where he developed rheumatic fever. From childhood he suffered from a difficulty in pronouncing his R's and S's, which was corrected by surgery.

He studied acting at the Central School of Speech and Drama in the 1950's. Denied the right to use his last name by his father, who hated actors, Jeremy selected the name Brett from a suit label, a serendipitous choice, for Brett obviously plays better than Huggins, but then almost anything plays better than Huggins.

In 1956 he married Anna Massey, of the acting Massey family, sired a son, David, but was divorced from her in 1963.

Brett played on the English stage, but also appeared in films, the first being the Hollywood production of *War and Peace* in 1956. He sought the role of James Bond but was not chosen, and thereafter joined the prestigious National Theatre Company of Laurence Olivier. He played in *Hedda Gabler* and *My Fair Lady*, touring in *The Tempest* and as the lead in *Dracula*. He appeared in television in *Rebecca* and in *The Good Soldier*.

These television dramas were put on by Masterpiece Theater, whose producer was Joan Wilson, a talented and beautiful lady whom I remember from Grinnell College days. In 1976 Brett became her fourth husband and she his second wife, and like Rathbone and his wife and Gillette and his, it became the most overwhelming relationship in his life. For Brett, it was a companionate marriage at first, and one of the reasons for it was to permit Brett to obtain a green card. The second marriages of both Rathbone and Brett were the most sustaining thing in each of their lives, as was Gillette's only marriage, even when it ended in her early death.

Joan Brett was an exceptionally strong woman, much stronger than her husband, and he relied greatly upon her — he called her his confidence — and her death from cancer resulted in his breakdown in 1986. He once said that "without her there was no reason to go on."[1]

So far as I have been able to determine, Brett is the only actor who has played both Holmes and Watson, playing the latter to Charlton Heston's Holmes in *Crucifer of Blood* on Broadway in 1980. But it was as Holmes in the Granada series which gained him far more than a transient fame. The first episode of the *Adventures* was shown in Britain in the Spring of 1984, and like the other two portrayers of Holmes, he was accepted, not uncritically, but critically and enthusiastically. For many he was the quintessential Holmes, emphasizing a certain Holmesian instability. The emphasis was not unintentional as Brett was himself possessed by the demon of instability. I have long believed that Holmes was a manic depressive and as Brett himself suffered from the same terrible condition, the fit of actor and character was that of a gloved hand. Someone once suggested to Brett in a telephone interview that Holmes suffered from this very condition, whereupon Brett said nothing but threw the telephone down.[2] Brett later went public with his condition in a nation-wide appeal for the society dedicated to assisting those with this tragic illness.

But he had another, more secret problem, the existence of which afflicted him, causing him great internal turmoil. According to the author, Terry Manners, in his recent biography,[3] Brett roiled from being bisexual. Brett regarded this as an affliction, apparently never coming to terms with it in his troubled life.

Davies, his biographer based on the Granada productions, saw him in the clutches of the disease, when he remarked on "the sudden snarl, the icy remark and the cruel rejection… the classic behavior of the manic depressive."[4]

But there was more to the Brett interpretation than illness. One of the directors of the Granada series, Paul Annett, described Brett as "a little crazy, wonderfully eccentric at times…(a)nd like a lot of actors, he was basically insecure."[5] Brett himself saw in Holmes a dark and mysterious character, and a complicated one at that. Brett's portrayal showed a Holmes who was all of these things, although Brett's condition caused him more problems than did Holmes' condition. Indeed, as the series advanced Brett became a more distraught Holmes. He developed lithium poisoning and heart problems, all of which affected his Holmes characterization.

Like Rathbone, he developed a dislike of Holmes. He once said that "I never liked the devil from the start. I can't find anything of me in him. I must learn to live again."[6] At the tenth anniversary party for the Granada Holmes series, Brett told the group that he could not play Holmes any longer. "Holmes is the hardest part I have ever played — harder than Hamlet or Macbeth. You see, everyone, Holmes has become the dark side of the moon for me. He is moody and solitary and underneath I am really sociable and gregarious. It has all got too dangerous. I should have played Bambi right from the start."[7]

The haircut which he inflicted on himself, and which appears in the series, was explained by his Watson and friend, Edward Hardwick, the son of the celebrated Sir Cedric Hardwick:

> "Jeremy just got into one of his manic states — you know, I hate Sherlock Holmes etc., and one day he cut his hair. In front of the mirror he lopped bits off..."[8]

Despite his mental problems, which on occasion required hospitalization, he was able, on occasion, to evidence his essential sense of humor, something which the sardonic Holmes clearly lacked. David Burke, his first Watson, related how Brett told him that he was so depressed that he sent himself a fan letter, which contained the statement that none of the other Holmes portrayers were fit to clean his boots, and assuring himself that the term magic was the only appropriate one to describe his performances as Holmes. The fan letter also requested a signed photograph. Burke, bemused, inquired if he really mailed it to himself, and was assured that he had, affixing a first class stamp as he was anxious to receive it.

Burke asked if he had sent the photograph to himself, and Brett responded that of course he had not, since he was not barking mad, as "the bugger didn't send a stamped addressed envelope."[9]

Like Rathbone, Brett half-feared that Holmes would end by possessing him. Brett said during his American tour that "Some actors fear if they play Sherlock Holmes for a very long run the character will steal their soul, leave no corner for the original inhabitant — and when the role ends, leave them unable to act without a pipe and a deerstalker cap."[10] He once told a reporter that Holmes "is such a giant. Such a genius, such a bore, such...an isolated, damaged penguin — I hate him. Every time I nearly get there he escapes me again."[11]

Brett's own valedictory to Holmes was eloquent and his own words should be offered as a conclusion.

> The only thing I do have in common with Sherlock Holmes is a kind of enthusiasm, mine is for life, his is for work. He's dead when he's not working — in that sense he is like an actor. But I've had a fascinating time playing him. I said to Dame Jean that I've danced in the moonlight with your father for ten years. The moonlight, not the sunlight — Holmes is a very dark character.[12]

NOTES

1. Davies, David Stuart, *Bending the Willow*, Calabash Press, Penyffordd, Chester, 1996.
2. *Ibid,*, page 80.
3. Manners, Terry, *The Man Who Became Sherlock Holmes, The Tortured Mind of Jeremy Brett* (Virgin Books: London, 1997).
4. *Ibid.*, page 85.
5. *Ibid.*, page 43.
6. *Ibid.*, page 94.
7. Manners, cited supra, p. 212.
8. *Ibid.*, page 94.
9. *Ibid.*, pages 182, 183.
10. Manners, cited supra, p. 216.
11. Manners, cited supra, p. 184.
12. *Ibid.*, page 179.

The Myth

WE HAVE NOW CONSIDERED certain people who had their being in time, and from whose lives emananated certain currents, for good or ill, which touched the lives of others.

We have seen how Doyle, with all the cunning of his craft, created a tapestry which presented together the real and the fancied, intermingling fact and fiction into one seamless web. It is a tight little universe of its own, complete and compelling, full of essential reality, standing, as the old legal writers wrote, on its own bottom, or in their later variant, on all fours. All of which is to say that the Holmesian world was convincing and balanced, and so it has entered a life of its own, all because a master literary craftsman, even mightily bored with his creation, can still produce magic. And magic was what Doyle produced in the Canon.

A minor theme of this book has been the development of the miracle plays and their historic successors, the melodramas (including the Marlowe and Shakespeare plays), and their successors, the nineteenth century novels with their subspecies, the mysteries. The Canon is the lineal and linear descendant of these progenitors, but with a certain literary twist which Doyle devised: the serial with separate stories but with one continuing central character. It was a masterstroke which made Doyle a wealthy man and constituted a new art form, still utilized successfully a hundred years hence. Undoubtedly its vitality will carry it forward for another few hundred years.

Doyle's other creation was a character, that of Mr. Sherlock Holmes, who — one cannot surely say which —

together with the standard central character and the serial art form of separate stories, also createdf by him, remain as current now as when they were born.

The Holmes stories carry within them an essential element of the miracle plays, which is the problem of evil. Until recent years, it was a popular thesis that evil, masquerading as crime, was the result of the circumstances of poverty, and that the social technicians, still loudly around, could erase poverty and thus crime and therefore an iniquitous form of evil. The devil did not prosper. God was abundantly good, the world was essentially good, and there was an upward and onward mobility of and in history. Solutions abounded: Marx would destroy the capitalist classes so that the worker's paradise would spring into being; the liberals would abolish poverty and all other problems by a benevolent government; and Emile Coue would accomplish personal perfection by people repeating the litany that in every day and in every way they were getting better and better. Dr. Graham would accomplish good health with his crackers and Dr. Kellogg with his cereals. It was to be a perfect world, free of evil and therefore constituting the equivalent of the exorcism of the devil. Our perception of our world can no longer be so simplistic.

Doyle understood that as there was good, so must there also be evil. He also knew that evil abounded. The duality of the world bothered him, and he found peace in Spiritualism. But he was a giant literary craftsman and he knew that not even Holmes could forever exorcise the devil, so there was the malignity of evil in the stories. Doyle limned a true universe, and while evil therefore existed, it was never unmitigated nor unmingled with good.

But if Doyle accepted evil as a necessary part of the human condition, he did not enjoy it, and there was a mechanism for redressing it — Mr. Sherlock Holmes, the avenger. When Holmes failed because he was, after all, mortal, the escaping malefactors could not escape the vengeance of their fates. Think how many times the miscreants embarked on vessels never to be heard from again or how often vengeful women in foreign cities wreaked their revenge. So if the devil never really died, neither, however, did the ancient concept of Nemesis.

In the Holmes stories, like the miracle plays and the melodramas, evil was abundantly present, but it did not prevail; and it made no difference if it manifested itself in the powerful or the weak; the result was always the same. There was measured and inevitable retribution.

But evil is a serious subject, and both the miracle plays and the melodramas recognized that the leaven of a good yarn was necessary to carry the burden of the message. Doyle did not set out to analyze evil, as other nineteenth century authors like Dickens did, but he did recognize that evil had its arresting qualities, and could compel the reader's attention. However, as Doyle was a gentleman, evil could not triumph. So it would be that it was Moriarty who would ultimately perish; certainly not Holmes.

And so also was it that the mythical figure of Sherlock Holmes would always stand, as he still stands, not juxtaposed, but interposed, between his clients and evil, and he would providentially prevail. Holmes was not a gentleman, but he possessed, generally, a gentleman's code, because it was also Doyle's code. So if evil entered the Canon, as it did the miracle plays of its predecessors, so also did the valiant youth, the importuned maiden, the faithful friend, and all the other archetypical figures from the ancient mythic past of man.

That is why Holmes lives. That is why Holmes will live.

Afterword

THE TAPESTRY OF THE CANON is interwoven with a myriad of real people. Some were identifiable when written and they continue to be identifiable, although somewhat blurred by time.

It is interesting that many of the non-real people within the confines of the Canon have developed a reality of their own; and more than that, a reality greater than that of the real people. This is not surprising, as the incredible cavalcade of characters in the Canon have been limned by the master hand of a superb writer, Arthur Conan Doyle. What is even more interesting, is that Doyle soon came to hate the Holmes stories and Holmes himself, yet despite this, he continued to create believable people and generally believable plots. This is so because even the hack writing of a master can breathe with immortality.

The Canon, in my view, will come to be regarded someday as the great novel of the nineteenth century, despite strong competition from the brilliant works of the Brontes, Melville, Balzac, Tolstoy, and Dostoyevsky, for it is panoramic and mighty, offering a whole society to our convenient scrutiny. And I suspect that someday, for that same reason, it will be regarded as having as its closest kin Don Quixote's picaresque adventures.

There is an argument from authority which can be made here. John Betjeman, the then English Poet Laureate, wrote to his friend, Ian Fleming, late in their friendship, "The Bond world is as real and full of fear and mystery as Conan Doyle's Norwood and Surrey and Baker Street. I think the only other person to have invented a world in our time is Wodehouse."

But long views are easily offered because they cannot be disproved when presented, and when the rub comes, the provider of the view is long dead. Yet we know what has happened in the last hundred years to the sixty Holmes stories, and who could have predicted that what was considered ephemera would have such a life? Certainly not even Doyle, to his discomfiture.

As William Bolitho once wisely observed, the Holmes stories are about "a town and a time," but they are more than social archeology. They have vitality and they possess truth. That is what counts.

Some claim that popular fiction will never live, but Somerset Maugham knew and articulated the truth that no writing will last unless it initially enters the published world. And after passing through the gate of popular fiction, who knows? Each generation offers its own assessment, based upon its own particular value system. Consider, as a case in point, the reaction of the readers to *The Great Gatsby*, which has advanced from being regarded as a frivolous set-piece about silly people in an absurd time to a recognition that perhaps it is the greatest American novel of this century, as was *Moby Dick*, albeit belatedly, so regarded for the last century.

We cannot tell from the work itself who was real in the Canon and who was not. Isn't that the ultimate test of a mighty book?

Doyle understood many things, some of them very difficult in conception, but he never did appreciate what he had wrought. If he was right about immortality, then he now realizes that it was his most trivial work — or so he regarded it — which has become a vital part of the heritage of the entire world; and it is a work laced with errors because he did not regard it as worth his time and trouble to remember the consistency. And all of his serious work in historical fiction with its carefully crafted historicity — which he counted on for his remembered reputation — lacks the dignity of even being a footnote today, while his money grubbing hack stuff (of which our sainted Holmes is the prime example) lives and will continue to live, all of which establishes that a great writer can write greatly even when he does not intend to do so.

The ancient Greeks believed that perfection in anything belonged only to the gods — so it was that every Greek work of art contained a slight but quite deliberate flaw. Perhaps that is the justification for what we regard as Canonical errors.

But the Canon is read not because of its intrinsic artistic merit but because it is great fun, although Britons and Americans still labor under the odd belief that there cannot be greatness hiding within what is enjoyable. Greatness, it seems to some, can surface only in what is heavy and complicated, reeking of the profound. In fact, it was a Briton who once said that the Briton most appreciates the person with little talent who is very modest about it. Doyle had a great talent but he was also very modest about it, which is probably why he is more enjoyed than appreciated.

In any event, quite apart from the critical analyses of the *cognoscenti*, whose most damning criticism of any work is that it is "popular," Mr. Sherlock Holmes and company will long endure, offering solace to the afflicted and pleasure to all. There is a trenchant Arab saying, rendered in English, that the dogs bark but the caravan moves on.

To possess Holmes is a delight. Just as he possesses us, we possess him. It is a self-enforcing exchange, but it is more, for it is an elixir. A dram or two of Sherlock is invariably a very special medicine indeed; and it is a prescription to be taken liberally as needed.

Bibliography

1 — THE SORCERER
Doyle, A. Conan, *Memories and Adventures*, Little, Brown & Co., Boston, 1924
Liebow, Ely M., *Dr. Joe Bell, Model for Sherlock Holmes*, Bowling Green University, Bowling Green, OH, 1982
Pond, Maj. J.B., *Eccentricities of Genius*, Dillingham, New York, 1900

2 — THE SORCERER'S APPRENTICE
Doyle, A. Conan, *Memories and Adventures*, Murray, London, 1930
Hammer, David L.,*The Worth of the Game*, Gasogene Press, Dubuque, 1993
Hammer, David L.,*The Before Breakfast Pipe*, Gasogene Press, Dubuque, 1995
Liebow, Ely M., *Dr. Joe Bell, Model for Sherlock Holmes*, Bowling Green University Popular Press, Bowling Green, OH, 1982
Smith, Cuthbert, *Watson's Son Reveals Real Sherlock Holmes*, Des Moines Register, January 16, 1938

3 — THE HERO
Bunbury, *Narrative of Passages in the Late War in France*, London, 1854
Dictionary of National Biography,
Johnstone, Chevalier, *Memoirs*

4 — THE HEROINE I
Brough, James, *The Prince & the Lily*, Coward, McCann & Geoghegan, New York, 1975
Gerson, Noel B.,*Because I Loved Him, The Life and Loves of Lillie Langtry*, William Morrow & Company, New York, 1971
Harrison, Michael, *Fanfare of Strumpets*, W.H. Allen, London, 1971
Sichel, Pierre, *The Jersey Lily, The Story of the Fabulous Mrs. Langtry*, Prentice Hall, Englewood Cliffs, 1958

5 — THE HEROINE II
Harrison, Michael, *Fanfare of Strumpets*, W. H. Allen, London, 1971

Lewis, Arthur H.,*La Belle Otero*, Trident Press, New York, 1967
Skinner, Cornelia Otis, *Elegant Wits and Grand Horizontals*, Houghton Mifflin, Boston, 1962

6—THE KING
Hammer, David L. *A Royal Client: Being a Scandal in Bulgaria*, SHJ, Vol. 18, No.3, Winter, 1987
Hammer, David L., *The Before Breakfast Pipe of Mr. Sherlock Holmes*, Gasogene Press, Ltd., Dubuque, 1995

7—THE QUEEN
Gernsheim, Helmut & Alison, *Victoria R*, G.P. Putnam, New York, 1959
Hibbert, Christopher, *Queen Victoria in her Letters and Journals*, Viking, New York, 1985
Ponsonby, Sir Frederick, *Recollections of Three Reigns*, Eyre & Spottiswoode, London, 1954
Sitwell, Edith, *Victoria of England*, Houghton Mifflin, Boston, 1936
Strachey, Lytton, *Queen Victoria*, Harcourt, Brace and Company, New York, 1921
Weintraub, Stanley, *Victoria*, Talley/Dutton, New York, 1987
Woodham-Smith, Cecil, *Queen Victoria*, Alfred A. Knopf, New York, 1972

8—THE JUDGE
Hammer, David L., *The Worth of the Game*, Gasogene Press, Dubuque, 1993

9—THE VILLAIN
Dressler, David, *The Little King of Crime*, Coronet Magazine, December 1948, Vol. 25/No. 2, pages 98-102
Felstead, S. Theodore, *Shades of Scotland Yard*, John Long Ltd., London
Horan, James D., *The Pinkertons: The Detective Dynasty That Made History*, Crown Publishers, New York, 1969
Kohn, G., *Dictionary of Culprits and Criminals*, Scarecrow Press, Metuchen, NJ, 1986
Macintyre, Ben, *The Napoleon of Crime,The Life and Times of Adam Worth, The Real Moriarty*, Harper Collins, London, 1997
Nash, Jay Robert, *Encyclopedia of World Crime*, Crime Books, Wilmette, IL, 1990
Rowan, Richard Wilmer, *The Pinkertons, a Detective Dynasty*, Little, Brown and Company, Boston, 1931

10—THE MAIDEN
Belford, Barbara, *Violet*, Simon and Schuster, New York, 1990

Cooper, Diana, *Autobiography*, Carroll & Graf, New York, 1988
Cooper, Diana, *The Rainbow Comes and Goes*, Houghton Mifflin, New York, 1958
Hardwick, Joan, *Immodest Violet*, Andre Deutsch, London, 1990
Lambert, Angela, *Unquiet Souls*, Harper & Row, New York, 1984
Masters, Brian, *The Dukes*, Blond and Briggs, London, 1977
Whibley, Charles, *Lord John Manners and His Friends*, Wm. Blackwood, Edinburgh, 1925
Zeigler, Philip, *Diana Cooper*, Book Club Assoc., London, 1981

11—THE PREMIER

Encyclopedia Britannica, volumes 3, 10, 16, 19, Chicago, 1966
Jenkins, Roy, *Gladstone*, Random House, New York, 1997
Minney, R.J.,*No, 10 Downing Street; A House in History*, Little Brown & Co.,Boston, 1963
Wilson, Harold, *A Prime Minister on Prime Ministers*, Summit Books, New York, 1977

12—THE PRINCE

Aronson, Theo, *The King in Love*, Harper & Row, New York, 1988
Brook-Shepherd, Gordon, *Uncle of Europe*, Collins, London, 1975
Cowles, Virginia, *Gay Monarch; The life and Pleasures of Edward VII*, Harper & Brothers, New York, 1956
Hibbert, Christopher, *The Royal Victorians*, J.P. Lippincott, Philadelphia, 1976
Pearsall, Ronald, *Edwardian Life and Leisure*, St. Martins Press, New York, 1973

13—THE DUKE

Masters, Brian, *The Dukes*, Blond and Briggs, London, 1977
Pearson, John, *The Serpent and the Stag*, Holt, Rinehart & Winston, New York, 1983
Whibley, Charles, *Lord John Manners and His Friends*, 2 vols, Wm Blackwood, Edinburgh, 1925
Ziegler, Philip, cited *supra*

14—THE DEVIL'S APPRENTICE I

Birkenhead, Earl of, *Famous Trials*, Hutchinson & Co., London
Honeycombe, Gordon, *The Murders of the Black Museum*, Hutchinson, London, 1982
Scott, Sir Harold, *Scotland Yard*, Andre Deutsch, London, 1954
Shore, Teignmouth, *Trials of Charles Frederick Peace*, Hodge, Edinburgh. 1926

15—THE DEVIL'S APPRENTICE II
Angeli, Helen Rossetti, *Pre-Raphaelite Twilight*, The Richards Press, London, 1954
Belford, Barbara, *Violet*, cited *supra*
Winwar, Frances, *Poor Splendid Wings*, Little, Brown & Co, Boston, 1933

16—THE VALLEY OF VERMISSA
Hammer, David L., *To Play The Game*, Gasogene Press Ltd, Dubuque, 1991

17—THE EXODUS
Ibid.

18—THE PROMISED LAND
Ibid.

19—THE GREAT-HEARTED SOLDIER
British Medical Journal, page 557, 1907
Hammer, David L., *The Worth of the Game*, Gasogene Press, Dubuque, 1993
The London Gazette, November 19, 1880
Letter of J.O. Campbell, R.A.M.C. Historical Museum, Aldershot, Hants, England, dated 13 February 1984, to the author

20—THE CONNECTICUT CONNECTION
Baker Street Miscellanea, No. 29, Spring, 1982,(Gillette Issue)
Gillette, William, *Sherlock Holmes: A Play*, Halbach, Helen, Santa Barbara, 1974
Hammer, David L., *To Play the Game*, Gasogene Press, Dubuque, 1991
Stone, P.M., *William Gillette's Stage Career*, BSJ, Vol. 12, No.1, page 8, 1962.

21—THE LITERATE PORTRAYER
Rathbone, Basil, *In and Out of Character*, Doubleday & Company, Garden City, 1962

22—THE MOONLIGHT PORTRAYER
Davies, David Stuart, *Bending the Willow*, Calabash Press, Penyfford, Chester, 1996